MORE THAN MILLIONS

MORE THAN MILLIONS

FINDING THE GOLD WITHIN

STORIES TO SPARK POSSIBILITY, ABUNDANCE AND UNSHAKABLE TRUST

Marcia Maizel-Clarke

FOUNDER OF DOGEARED JEWELRY

TSPA

THE SELF PUBLISHING AGENCY

Marcia Maizel-Clarke
More than Millions: Finding the Gold Within

Dogeared Media
Copyright 2026 by Marcia Maizel-Clarke
First Edition

Hardcover ISBN 979-8-9987899-0-8
Softcover ISBN 979-8-9987899-1-5
eBook ISBN 979-8-9987899-2-2
Audiobook ISBN 979-8-9987899-3-9

Cover Concept and Art Direction | Grace Clarke
Cover & Interior Design Production| Danna Mathias Steele
Editor | Debra Evans
Copy Editor | Kathie Lynas
Author Portrait Photography | Grace Clarke
Publishing Management | TSPA The Self Publishing Agency, Inc.

To my Merlin . . . Our love affair has allowed me to fly and to fall with grace and ease. Because of you and your love, I am always able to dust myself off and get ready for my next, next.

To my kids, Grace and Jordan . . . My heart is bolder, fuller, and happier because of getting to be your mom. Thanks for choosing me. YOU are the cool kids.

To my parents . . . Thank you for sticking with me. I did pave my own way, and I know that was not always easy. You show us even more today what being a loving family means.

CONTENTS

FOREWORD

Caftans. We both love them. Flowing, effortless, and perfect for staying above it all while still getting things done.

Our daughters are close in age. And coincidentally, I went to high school with one of her best friends from college. Small world.

But beyond that, Marcia and I didn't have much in common when I started working for her jewelry company Dogeared as a part-time assistant in 2008, eventually becoming the creative director. That became obvious the day she smudged the office. I thought we were testing the smoke alarms. Or when she casually rattled off mantras—mantras!—that later became a bestselling jewelry collection. Who actually walks around telling themselves they're worthy, loved, and fearless?

Marcia does.

I have never met anyone like her. She can see an entire bracelet line in a basic piece of string. A simple circle necklace paired with a message about karma? Boom—over a million sold.

She doesn't do the word *no*. Or *can't*. Or *eventually*.

She operates on expansion, opportunity, and abundance.

Yes, in her people-first approach, she remains the self-proclaimed hippie who started stringing beads at her kitchen table. But in business? She's as solid as an oak tree—deeply rooted in her core beliefs, and resilient enough to handle numbers, vendors, customers, and challenges of every size.

Marcia built something transformative, and she did it her way. Today, she continues to run the company as it continues to evolve. This book? It's your peek inside her mind.

Buckle up.

If you're expecting a step-by-step business manual, this isn't it. Instead, it's a story about creating, allowing, and having *more*. More success, fulfillment, and joy—but also the freedom to continually redefine what "more" means to you in business and life.

Marcia shares her journey from selling jewelry at the Rose Bowl Flea Market just outside of Los Angeles, to creating an entirely new category in the industry: charm necklaces packaged with messages that spoke to people in a way jewelry never had.

Make a wish.
Accomplish magnificent things.
What goes around comes around.
Big things start with three little wishes.
True friends are like anchors.
You're never alone. Your guardian angel is always with you.

These aren't just taglines. They're affirmations people need. Through Marcia's vision, jewelry became a vehicle for connection, milestones, and daily reminders of self-worth.

But growing a business isn't just about the big wins. It's also about navigating the messy middle—manufacturing, merchandising, branding, and, most challenging of all, *people.* Some will lift you up. Some will let you down. You can have the best systems in the world, but ultimately, it's the humans who make or break your company. Marcia has seen it all—the loyalty, the love, the betrayal, the lessons.

This book is not about overnight success. It's about grit, heart, hustle, and the sheer stubbornness it takes to build something that over three decades has employed hundreds, and produced meaningful pieces worn on necks and wrists across the world.

You'll see the entire picture—the love story that gave birth to a multi-million dollar business, the money-making ideas and the costly ones, the bold strokes and intricate details of operating a business where production parts can be as small as the eye of a needle. The personal health crisis. The unwavering family and friends who made all the difference.

Get ready to nod your head, laugh, and maybe even re-think how you view success—both in business and in life.

Mimi Ison
Creator of the *Hey Middle Age* community and blog
2025

INTRODUCTION

Since you've picked this book up and are considering it for your next read, I say, yes please, and thank you. You are the reason I have put pen to paper and the motivation for sharing the stories and lessons learned that I offer here.

No one tells you when you start to write a book that the title of said book might be the very last piece of the puzzle to fall into place. *More than millions sold, loved, and worn*—this marketing tag line, describing a milestone in the business I started with my husband, was the motivating sentence that led to the title of this book. And that's exactly as it needed to be, as you will discover here.

More than millions sold, loved, and worn.

Ruminating on that line, the word "more" began to unfurl in my heart and mind like a flower in full bloom. Not "more" in an accounting sort of way, a simple tallying up of numbers, but as a reminder of life's infinite abundance and generosity. There is always *more!* "More" was suddenly the spark of inspiration that I needed! Yes, technically it describes a particular marker of business success we had reached, but more importantly it speaks to where we are *all* always going next . . . in business, in life, and in love. Life lavishes us with more beauty and grace when we're willing to receive it (and sometimes even when we're not willing).

As for inspiration, I think we need it like we need oxygen and water. We especially look for inspiration when we are feeling ready to go to the "next level" in our own story. For me, the many walks and talks with my friends are definitely among the most amazing (and cherished) ways that "more" shows up—and are a huge part of how I move through my life, and even the next-level reality that is this book.

It was *time* for this book. And sharing the process with my friends turned old doubts into clarity and excitement!

Maybe you've arrived at a place in your life now where it's time! Maybe you are looking for more creative inspiration, financial overflow, romantic fire, and spiritual connection. Through the stories, perspectives, and lessons learned woven throughout this book, my intention is that *More than Millions* may open new doors of possibility and abundance in your heart, your mind, and your life. That it be a place for you where your realities find support and you make contact with the unlimited world that's already in play.

REINVENTION ANYONE?

As I was writing this book, I turned sixty. I asked myself, *What does my age—this age—inspire in me? How much fun and adventure can I stir up in my daily life (and maybe even in the wider world)? How do I focus on what I want, even when our collective gravitational pull is to spend time on things that don't matter.* I don't think it was coincidental that around this same time, my husband Merlin and I began the process of re-imagining our company, Dogeared Jewelry. We founded Dogeared over thirty years ago and have grown up with our customers, our employees, and their families. As a business we started as a carefree young couple, before becoming parents of two, Dogeared illuminated a footpath through life that I could not have dreamed of in my twenties. It's been a wabi-sabi journey of our own making that has given us everything. It has provided a huge extended family, opportunities to be of service to our local community and beyond, a canvas for ongoing creative expression, and the means to create and share wealth. As you'll discover in the pages to come, Dogeared has been a kind of temple of love and gratitude disguised as a business.

In this reinvention process, Merlin and I have prioritized the projects that feel most aligned with who we are becoming, which also happen to be the things we're most excited about. I think it's a good practice in general to follow your trails of excitement and see where they lead. For us, this includes the Healing Bus (which I'll tell you all about in Chapter 2), a documentary we are in the process of defining, publishing this book, and creating new ways to connect with our community and ourselves. Creativity and curiosity are in the house as this rebranding journey takes us down new roads that we could not have imagined many moons ago. We are trusting in this process and this experience, as we know from experience that the "experience" is the secret sauce. Doing it all with an attitude of "finding the gold within" is a concept we are devoted to in our lives—and so it naturally became a golden thread woven throughout these pages.

DOGEAR THOSE PAGES!

One of the other themes here is about *revisiting* the past while *re-envisioning* the future—and loving big on them both. If you think about it, this is what happens when we dogear the pages of a book. Something has sparked our interest or holds great meaning for us in the now, and we want to be able to return to it with ease, later. Our hope is that having access to these self-selected passages will add to a deeper, richer, and more inspired experience of living. When we fold down the corner of a printed page, by putting in that crease we become curious collectors—of a story, a conversation, something that made us laugh, some advice that resonates, or an insight that struck deep. It's in this spirit that I have curated stories that make up *More than Millions*. They are from both the early days of building a life and a business to my world now. My stories and Dogeared's stories—my version, my truths, and "pearls of wisdom" gathered along the way—are woven together here, all into one multi-faceted love affair with family, friends, colleagues, and other collaborators. A love story about building a global brand that allows us to lend a hand to our local community and far beyond it. A love story about doing *and* being—where *Doing* falls head over heels with *Being*.

If I were to wave a wand and "Make a Wish" (one of our best-selling jewels), it would be this: that each of these stories encourages you to pursue your goals and dreams (whether brand new or long-held), that they lift you up, and maybe even make you laugh. I want this collection of chapters to support the idea that you get to create all the unlimited opportunities ahead, and to *move* you to trust in yourself, and your actions, and the universal flow that supports each of our lives . . . to discover an *unshakable* trust within. This book, in the eyes of the traditional publishing industry, is not categorized strictly as a "how-to" business guide or self-help book or even a memoir. It's a true hybrid, and I like it that way. It suits me if it defies categorization because I want this book to touch your life in the ways that matter to you. (Who knows, maybe for you it'll feel more like the romance genre ☺.)

LUCKY NUMBER SEVEN

Over time, I've noted the recurring themes, patterns, and ideals at the heart of Dogeared Jewelry. Ultimately, I distilled a long list down to seven principles that are my dear and trustworthy guides—The Seven. The principles that most remind me how to live in flow at every turn, especially when I find myself in moments of fear or uncertainty and am looking for a way out! In their own ways, each is a pillar that supports the concept of "finding the gold within."

1. Lead with Love (Self-Love especially)
2. Rock a "No Problem" Attitude
3. Choose Your Lens; It's the Life You Will Lead
4. Be Present
5. Value and Hold on Tight to Self-Care and Health
6. Circulate Good
7. Trust in Divine Timing and Divine Guidance

My truths, these seven principles, which are outlined in full in Chapter 1, are woven throughout this book. Some of them may resonate more strongly for you than others. If so, take these energetic attractions as signs—signs for you to consider something in a new way, or to motivate action, or to remember what matters most to you. Sometimes the sign will be a gentle reminder that the wisdom you seek is already within you.

Marcia Maizel-Clarke
Spring 2025

PROLOGUE

SHE

"She." Her pronoun is "she." She is a powerful healer. She represents true love and loyalty. Lessons in all areas of my life have come through her. She is aligned with all things good and is committed to connecting with people this way. She has graciously allowed me to create and make something with her that helps the world. She can be tough, and the ride can be bumpy. Her integrity is fierce, and she doesn't back down. She can be unexpected. Her energy is magnetic, and lots of people want her attention. She has a language style that is bold, sweet, direct, connected, and positive. She leads with kindness. She is very hard to be with sometimes, as her commitment to what she is here for is unwavering. Challenges can show up, but hindsight has given her the wisdom to realize that everything about her is necessary and perfect. She is shaped by the energy of everyone around her who cares for her in the best of ways. Her positive energy is contagious.

"She" is one of the great loves of my life.
"She" is Dogeared Jewelry.

I never woke up one day and said, "Let's create a jewelry company that will impact millions of people and help connect our global community to their own healing and power of believing." I would have laughed out loud, mostly as I never saw myself as anyone with the skill sets or confidence to do anything like this. Not being able to make a decision was my middle name. I am a six on the enneagram. I was a freedom-seeking, let's-have-fun sort of hippie-minded girl, a girl who just wanted to feel the energy of creative expression and sometimes be in service. I believed in my angel cards, and in love (I still do). I did not see myself getting married, or even having children, as I wanted to be freeeee . . .

Thirty-plus years later, with Merlin, I have been on a journey that I truly never saw coming. Dogeared reminds the community of all things good within themselves and emanates an energy that feels like a hug in times of need. Dogeared is goodness. She becomes personified by everyone who has been a customer, part of our team, or part of our community and tribe. She came to be, as she could not, not. It was her time, and as one who, with my whole heart, believes in divine timing, I am grateful as I have gotten to be the rider on the back of a beautiful mare that was ready to go, go, go. The ride of my life, which intuitively feels so clear and on purpose. And one that gives me pauses for gratitude every day.

This is our story. Experiencing and experimenting with an energy that is connected and powerful. Saying "yes" to all things "she" and more. Lessons learned, lessons learned again, and sometimes even again, and all the growth that comes with being human, in this extraordinary life school.

CHAPTER 1

FINDING THE GOLD WITHIN AND THE SEVEN

I am going to confess my obsession with circles. I love circles, symbolically and every other way. Women in circle is one of my favorite places to be. From cancer, to kids, to business, to dancing, to feeling unsure, to betrayal, to learning an ancient healing modality, to whatever shows up in my big ole circle.

Circling around in my life like this, it eventually became clear to me that there are certain truths that always guide my choices, both professionally and personally. In all, I identified the seven principles that I shared in the Introduction. These are the lighthouses that guide me, that I trust, which turned into the Dogeared philosophies in time. And, without fail, they empower me to go in search of and to find the gold within—to move from the conceptual into real-life discovery.

Empowerment is a mighty force. At its root, I believe it's the permission we give *ourselves* to move forward. While much

9

of what I want to share about this beautiful energy is best illustrated through the stories in this book, I hope you'll begin to sense and feel its life-giving force right here, right now. To be empowered is to give ourselves the green light to *act,* to take big leaps and baby steps—and to say "yes" to growth, evolution, and freedom. It's an exhilarating form of self-leadership. When we merge empowerment with trust—look out! Trust calls us to soften, to surrender, to open ourselves to life's flow—even when doubt, fear, or uncertainty cloud the way. Together, this becomes a living, breathing, and balanced force within us. It deepens over time, serving as both a wellspring of courage and a personal road map. And, perhaps most profoundly, it transforms us in the ways that matter. It supports us in finding the gold within and around us—internally, the wealth of time, experience, understanding, friendship, freedom, and love (including self-love); and externally, the money and other supportive resources we need and want.

In the chapters ahead, The Seven—a collection of values, perspectives, and emotional drivers—are illuminated through the stories and lessons learned that I hope will inspire you as you navigate your own path to further possibility, abundance, and unshakable trust. I am trusting that The Seven will also bring some of your own guiding lights even more clearly into view.

PRINCIPLE 1: LEAD WITH LOVE (ESPECIALLY SELF-LOVE)

What it's about: It begins with self-acceptance, acceptance of all your seasons and tides. Self-acceptance is at the heart of self-love. This kind of love opens the door to understanding that everyone has the capacity to feel loved and the superpower to ignite that feeling in another, even if for a moment.

Something you say or do (or don't do) can fan the flames for someone. It's an exchange of energy that starts with kindness. Kindness becomes your internal green light—it's about thinking the best of people, including yourself. It's about serving in this capacity even when you may not feel like it. Life happens in the present moment, and all these loving moments strung together become golden threads in the fabric of your tale. Each of us is a catalyst to change and to the energy we put out in the world. And when we lead with love of all kinds, we are, in effect, acknowledging that everyone wants to be seen, experienced, and received with an open heart, and it starts with you.

Principle 1 in action: Wear "love-colored glasses." Look in that mirror and talk to yourself and your body in a loving way. Daily. Hourly. Whatever works to start shifting the patterns we all carry that aren't rooted in kindness and compassion for ourselves. Speak to yourself as you would speak to your best friend.

"You are so beautiful."

"It's a really good hair day!"

"You are enough."

Maybe stand in front of a mirror so your words can mirror back to you. With practice, it will get easier and become a source of joy and power.

PRINCIPLE 2: ROCK A "NO PROBLEM" ATTITUDE

What it's about: It's about stopping in your tracks when you feel fear lurking around inside. When you are in fear, everything feels impossible. Stop the downward spiral and head straight into a solution-oriented frame of mind. A no drama, no chaos, "no problem!" mindset. Life is about interpretation, and you get to choose how you interpret and respond to all the comings, goings, events, and moments it holds. Approaching most encounters and experiences with a "no problem" orientation takes some of the power away from the fear and puts it back in your hands. This pivot toward a solution allows you to actually feel what you are feeling rather than be distracted by fear's game. And *all the feels* are important.

I love making "problem" just a word, one with no energy. I work to not use it in my vocabulary (except with a "no" in front of it). When I hear people start a sentence with the phrase "the problem is," I am always on guard, as I believe there is a solution not based in fear for most things, and I would rather start from that place. I believe we have two essential states to choose from in our lives: love or fear. In choosing love, we create a vibrancy that attracts love. Those are the vibes that I want to play with.

I was lucky to have some time in Bali where I experienced a constant state of "no problem." It's a beautiful, palpable feeling there. It's in the air and water. Merlin and I look at each other sometimes—when life feels like it's just too much—and say, "no problem," with the tone and smile in our eyes that we found within the Balinese people. Why not? It usually breaks the mental state and makes us laugh out loud. And laughing in my world is some powerful gold within. This doesn't mean everything is going to go our way; it means we get to choose to prioritize light and love and wrap all that around anything we may come upon during our day.

Principle 2 in action: *Practice using the powerhouse phrase "no problem" any time you have a negative thought, a challenging feeling (for example: fear, anxiety, doubt, anger), or a difficult encounter (whether mildly or strongly difficult). Optional: If you*

*feel inclined to sing along with me and Bob Marley, you can fol-
low up your declaration of "no problem" with "Every little thing
is gonna be all right."*

PRINCIPLE 3: CHOOSE YOUR LENS; IT'S THE LIFE YOU WILL LEAD

What it's about: It starts with acknowledging that your words
and thoughts have *so much* power to create and shape your reality.
It's intimately related to the other six principles because it's about
choosing how you're going to look at and meet each moment. You
get to choose, each minute of the day, which thoughts and feelings get to have an audience with you. When you are hurt and
angry, or you're not feeling heard or seen, it may take a beat to opt
out of negative self-talk and emotions, and it's so worth doing.
Holding on to negative emotions, like anger and its many shades
(resentment, bitterness, and rigidity, to name a few), for long periods of time only hurts you . . . and in all realms—spiritually,
emotionally, and physically. In short, it's about understanding
that choosing to be in a joyful place creates a joyful space. You are
who and what you surround yourself with, so choose well.

I engage in this principle multiple times a day. It's a chance
to practice the art of the reframe. It's also one of the hard-
est-working principles with the quickest, biggest bang! It's
my absolute favorite tonic for what I call the "50 shades of
nay." Inside of myself, I say *thank you: Thank you for my family,
thank you for my fingers that typed out this book, and thank you
for this computer. Thank you for the sunny day and for my healthy
body* . . . and the "ands" keep coming.

Principle 3 in action: *One minute of gratitude. Whenever you
feel some inner anxiety or resistance or dissatisfaction, stop for a*

moment and grab some gratitude. Say it out loud: "I am grateful for this cup of coffee, I am grateful the plant on my desk is happy and growing, I am grateful for the birds chirping through my window, I am grateful for having this time to be grateful. I am grateful to feel really good today" . . . and keep going. One minute of gratitude and your list will get creatively long and empowering.

PRINCIPLE 4: BE PRESENT

What it's about: First it's about feeling your connection with what is right here and right now. It's about remaining seated within your fine self even when your present moment is overflowing with the stuff of life—not abandoning yourself in pursuit of something or in avoidance of something else. It's about feeling, breathing, and receiving the gifts and messages that life is offering up. It's about being *available* for life—for the chance to give, to receive, to love and be loved. Yes, life and work are about the journey and not the arrival at some destination point. And the journey happens in and through presence—being awake and open to what is occurring in any given moment. A string of experiences. In presence, you can feel them, taste them, smell them, see them, hear them, and be with them.

Being present is the opposite of the "what if" orientation to life. Nothing else works as well as presence to keep that kind of mind chatter quiet. The stories we create in our minds about the future rarely come to fruition as expected, as the universe likes to surprise and delight. I can say with certainty that nothing is ever as I expect it. What a paradox! And when I work at being present—like right on top of my feet, here and now—the "what ifs" (many times, based in fear) melt away, and I experience life beautifully. I see the dolphins jumping in the ocean, I feel the sand under my feet, I actively listen to and hear my friend talk about her life, and my focus is not about anything more. So many times in my life, all I wanted to do was get from A to E with no thought to *enjoying* A, B, C, D, *or* E—a very common way of living that many of us get caught in. I vote that it's time to experience the whole alphabet!

Principle 4 in action: If you notice that you're not present or don't feel like being present, see if you can push the pause button on whatever you're doing and save it to do later when you can be present. This could be reading a text or email, making a phone call, watching a video link someone sent you, or taking care of something you need to do at home or work. Conversations will go better, your responses to others will be infused with greater clarity and connection, and people will feel seen, heard, and loved by your care. Your presence is a present!

PRINCIPLE 5: VALUE AND HOLD ON TIGHT TO SELF-CARE AND HEALTH

What it's about: It's about meditating, walking, getting enough sleep, breathing deeply, and spending time alone, as well as with friends and family. It's about self-expression, including writing, making music, and dancing. Sometimes it's about bodywork and acupuncture and salon visits. Most importantly, it's about making yourself a priority with no guilt and no shame around it. It's the care and feeding of you. Daily giving and receiving.

Understatement: This is not always easy. Many of us were brought up in a time when working hard to accomplish many things outside of ourselves was what success looked like. In this book, I will share a few stories that relate to this definition of success, including my superwoman period. I still feel like I have some superwoman qualities, yet this concept has been redefined for me as well. Having an "S" on my chest for superwoman is no longer something I strive for. Living with an "S" on my chest to keep self-care at the top of mind allows me to live full out. Health is E-V-E-R-Y-T-H-I-N-G!

My self-care routines today are flexible as long as they take care of my physical body, feed my soul, and fuel my curiosity about life. I love to enjoy a strong body and a strong spiritual practice, which I believe allows me to open more fully to all of life's magic. I do fall off the "everything healthy" boat, and now I have a foundation and framework for stepping back into practice, as with everything else that matters to me.

Principle 5 in action: Baby steps. Choose a self-care priority to focus on. Just one. It could be drinking plenty of water each day. It could be going to bed earlier than normal. (This one is my big one.) Maybe it's being off your phone for the whole night. Maybe it's also not turning it on again until you've done something for your inner world first, like five minutes with your eyes closed and doing some deep breathing, quieting your mind, or spending even a few minutes outside just gazing at the sky. Making these moments a priority, you will find that you want to spend even more time this way. It feels so empowering to take good care of ourselves. Our body, minds, and spirit are yelling hallelujah!

PRINCIPLE 6: CIRCULATE GOOD

What it's about: Circles and kindness, two of my favorites. A dynamic duo. Circulating good can be the simplest of actions—giving a compliment, holding someone's hand, listening to a friend, smiling at a stranger, or saying hello to someone on a walk. It can be bringing soup to a sick neighbor. It can be more involved actions as well, such as volunteering your time for an organization you feel passionate about or helping care for someone you love who needs support. In all instances, these are actions that can spark energetic wildfires of positivity—feelings of relief, optimism, hope, and possibility.

The ability to circulate goodness has been one of the biggest gifts of the Dogeared journey. Our jewels allow us to connect to people—with good words, good actions, good intentions in action, just being in the circle of good. It has been our guiding light as we reimagine and reshape what is ahead for us professionally and personally.

And the light keeps getting brighter and brighter, revealing new doors to walk through that we didn't know were there just a little while ago. These revelations may be among the most powerful aspects of circulating good—the new horizons that come into view when caring for and connecting with each other.

Principle 6 in action: *Find simple ways to connect with others through giving. Here's one of my favorite, easy connections: When I am in line for tea/coffee/food, I give enough money to the cashier for the person behind me to get their order for free (or with a nice discount, depending on what they are ordering) without letting that person know. I usually turn to them and say, "Have a great day" and let the cashier deliver the surprise. This is most fun at a drive-through. I was the recipient of this type of gift on a trip to New Hampshire, during a Dunkin' Donuts coffee and tea run where I was the fourth person in the chain to receive! My contribution was the fifth one! I wanted to stay there and see if it kept going. So much fun for the cashier and a long-lasting inner smile for those of us who also got to play.*

PRINCIPLE 7: TRUST IN DIVINE TIMING AND DIVINE GUIDANCE

What it's about: It's about understanding that there is a time and space for everything, and it's all orchestrated for us. We get to trust that the universe is rooting for us and is presenting the guidance and gifts in the timing needed for our growth along the journey. I have lived a life in which I've worked on trusting in both divine timing and divine guidance, and I would have to say that as a principle to be practiced, this is one of the harder ones. When I feel like things are taking too long, I get to remember that I probably have more time than I think, and instead of being in the hurry up mode, my focus could be on enjoying the journey that I am in. This depth of trust is one of the most powerful ways to live. The guidance—from the universe, angels, source, God, or whatever fuels you—is there. It's *always* there and always accessible; you just gotta trust.

Talk to your source of sacred guidance out loud or in your quietness, whatever feels good to you. Ask questions, ask for signs, and look for playful, interesting ways to get your answers. Sometimes your answers are straightforward, like you clearly feel them or hear them. Sometimes they don't feel as direct. Either way, your answers do and will continue to present themselves in creative ways.

I communicate with my angels daily for everything in my life—which gives me great confidence to let go and know that I don't have to know! It can be for things little or grand. Our guides have time and space for it all. We chose to be here, in this life school, to practice, play, grow, and learn. To trust even *more* during the parts of the journey that are extra curvy and prickly is one of the great invitations—to know that higher forces are supporting you, *especially then*. Very much like Principle 6 (Circulate Good) above, this trust-filled orientation will open doors that you could not have imagined even existed in all parts of your life. Unshakable trust at its core.

Principle 7 in action: *This one is the easiest as it only requires* ***you*** *and a bit of quiet space. Using your voice out loud or using your internal voice, simply ask your divine team a question. If this is the first time, say hello, introduce yourself, and then continue to be still and notice what you hear or feel. Write it down. Your answer may not come right away, or it might be very clear immediately. Your practice with this will be your own. For me, I like to play a little. When I ask my questions out loud and then pull angel cards, I try to predict which cards I will pull. When I am right, my entire body buzzes. The more time you spend practicing, the easier it will get to receive the messages. Don't be attached to the outcome, especially when it relates to timing. As we have talked about, divine timing IS divine timing.*

There are so many ways that the concept of finding the gold within comes to life and takes form, and in the chapters and stories to come I believe you will be able to identify how it shows up for you now, how it could show up in your future, and what this could mean for you in your life, as it will manifest differently for everyone. For me, beautiful and connective relationships—foundational ones, including with myself—are key building blocks here, tuning me into wisdom that sometimes is not completely apparent in the physical realm. A universal connection that guides me somewhere, and often that place is one where I'm trusting myself.

Sometimes this great trust happens in the blink of an eye, and I cannot capture the how. Then I realize I don't need to understand or know the how—I just get to be present for the ride, with trust at the wheel.

OK, so now it's time to turn the page into the stories and moments where the principles of Chapter 1 have shown up and been in practice for me on my journey. I am grateful to share my perfectly imperfect path (in matters of business, partnership, family, friendship, health and wellness, spiritual growth, and more), so that you feel even greater self-permission to enjoy your unique path more than you ever imagined possible.

CHAPTER 2

PEARLS-IN-THE-PIE KIND OF LOVE

He gave me a beer. He gave my friend a beer. Thinking back, I am sure it was a Budweiser, as I know now that is what Merlin likes. At the party, we talked for a bit, until one of my friends, who was driving, was ready to leave as the guy she came to see was with someone else.

Merlin stood in front of my friend's car, wearing his Jimmy'z pants with a Velcro closure, a ripped Flash Dance T-shirt, and rockin' a serious mullet. It was the 80s and hair was expressive. My hair was big, really big. My nails were long and red. I wore a crop top showing my tan tummy, and there was lots of denim everywhere.

When he asked me for my phone number, I was unsure as to what to do. So, I did what every girl would do—I wrote down my number, crumpled it up, and threw it to him. Honestly, I wasn't interested in him and didn't expect to see him again.

When he called a few days later and asked to cook dinner for me, for some reason I said "yes." I seriously could not believe he called me. He seriously could not believe I wrote down my real number. I surprised myself because this was at a time in my life when I had decided not to date. Six months for just me. I was going to take time for self-care and see how it felt to be purposefully alone. I wasn't attracting the kind of man I thought I was ready for and wanted a change of focus. I was not a big dater, per se, but I did seem to have boyfriends more often than not. I loved being a couple. Even though I did not see myself married, I still wanted that person, that companion, that someone who would, in my mind at the time, make me feel whole and complete.

But what about my commitment to "not date right now," hmmm?

At the party, Merlin and I were together only fifteen minutes before I was pulled away. I had zero awareness that I had just met the man who would be the catalyst to so many incredible and unimaginable experiences in my life. I didn't know that he would be the one to show me love in all forms. He is the walker of the walk and talker of the talk.

Looking back, we laugh and say our angels were high-fiving each other. When Merlin meets Marcia. Fifteen minutes of pure divine timing. That is the start to our story, one that has spanned almost four decades.

FAST, SLOW, AND IN THE FLOW

Magical Merlin. His real name is Douglas, and he's a Boston boy to his core. He was dubbed Merlin when he was ten years old, a nod to Merlin Olsen, the celebrated football player, as Merlin's playing style was similar. The name Merlin suits him, and I know it was given to him as a gift, and as a container for all the alchemy he creates in the world.

Our love affair was slow, not immediate. We even broke up once for a short time. He was different from anyone I had ever dated. He was in the process of becoming a graphic designer, did not own a car, rode his bike everywhere, lived on the beach with two other women as roommates, had a big, happy dog named "Rugger," played rugby, and had the kindest, biggest heart of any human I had ever met. He was living his life from a place of freedom rather than fear, and that was something new to me. Money, prestige, and what other people were doing had no attachment to Merlin. Getting to know him, I found out that at a very young age, he read something in a book by Dr. Wayne Dyer that he recognized as his empowering truth—as his words to live by:

"There is no way to happiness. Happiness is the way."

My way at that time involved lots of travel, partying, aerobics classes with leg warmers, having fun, and not being too serious about anything. And somehow Marcia + Merlin matched up. Neither of us is too sure how it happened. We were in the flow, being present, and enjoying what was right in front of us.

When we moved in together just months after our first meeting, Merlin will tell you he did it because it made sense. He needed a roommate, and he loved me, so why not? I don't recall what I was thinking at that time, yet I am sure I was looking for more than a roommate who I loved. This was a big step for me, given the traditional way I was raised and that this was my first time living with a boyfriend. Living together changed everything for us. The more we shared, the more we realized we were each other's person.

Connecting with another human on a deep and meaningful level is an invitation to look at our own lives in a different way. We seemed naturally wired to support each other's passions, as well as help find those passions. We operated then, and still do, from a place that is dynamic and flowing. I believe this is key to any relationship, including the one we have with ourselves. Don't get stuck. Explore, be curious, trust in new things, and be open to the unlimited surprises that the world will offer if you are receptive to them. Doing this with another person allows for an even greater scope of experiences.

Marcia + Merlin had power to it. Knowing that I had my person who was there to prop me up, listen to me, or just hold space for whatever I needed gave me a kind of confidence to meet life with open arms. It provided the platform, forever more, to reach and stretch and fall and fly, and whatever else I wanted to do.

THE DEEPENING

During the holidays, Merlin and I help run one of the food/toy giveaways in the town of Compton for One Voice, an organization based in Santa Monica that has devoted more than forty years to supporting low-income families in the Los Angeles area, with all kinds of programming that will make you smile. We have been on the board of this organization as long as I have known Merlin. It's a grassroots nonprofit that we have grown up with that makes real life-changing impact. This particular annual event goes on for almost a week each year and always falls on my birthday. Participating in it is a family tradition, and one that we and our friends love and look forward to every holiday. After the main event, we always stop and eat somewhere to share thoughts about how it went, who we met, and recap our experience. During the "Year of the Pearls," as we call it, we stopped at a local coffee shop for some dessert. When I cut into my piece of blueberry pie with a fork, I had a huge surprise. I discovered a strand of pearls nestled inside. Merlin somehow had the diner staff get these pearls in there! This moment, and my feeling around all of it, is what makes my world go round. It's not past tense for me. It's soul delight in the now. And I want to live exactly like this and feel like this as much as possible. His creative generosity always leaves aftershocks of love, kindness, and feeling seen.

There was a thoughtfulness toward the other in this relationship that made it so different from anything I had experienced. I learned to always consider another person, which was a big growth area for me. At the same time, we were both independent and passionate, and many times I just wanted my own way, as did Merlin.

Merlin says I taught him how to "fight," which is not one of my proudest teachings. He was a gentle being who grew up never wanting to stress out his mom. He was from a family of five kids, so he was always working to be "that" guy, the one who did not stress anyone. When we were young, I had a lot of fire, and both of us always wanted to be right. Stubbornness is something we both embraced. When I look back, I realize we were learning how to communicate both well and not so well.

We got bumped around and bruised by the words that were said sometimes, as all couples do. We were figuring out and practicing how to be a couple, how to run a few businesses, and how to be with another person while still coming to know ourselves.

PEARLS OF WISDOM
I don't have to agree, AND I don't
have to be right. I am always willing
to apologize and move on.

As we are over thirty-five years into our relationship, most of our "fights" now do not include raising our voices or using words that hurt. One of my biggest learnings is that I do not have to be right. Period. Being right only supports the stubbornness that I am not interested in anymore. And it hurts my body and soul and takes up time and space in my mind that doesn't serve anything. It also isn't sustainable, as there are two of us, with very different orientations, and it's important to understand other viewpoints. I don't have to agree, *and* I don't have to be right. It works for us. Once I settle into that, where I can be with that paradox, I am always willing to apologize and move on. I think I can adopt this so easily because I know I am loved, and the foundation is there, so why not? At this point, most of our misunderstandings are us still working out our communication, which I believe will happen until we are no longer here on planet Earth. Typically, huge and powerful learnings come out of some of the "don't have to be right" times. It doesn't feel so great during the "learning," yet that hindsight evolving into wisdom is pretty good stuff.

QUESTION: *DO YOU WANT MORE?* ANSWER: *NOT YET*

Merlin had achieved his dream of becoming a graphic designer and was running a very lucrative design and advertising firm. I was proud of him and how he was using that creative mind of his every day to support his many clients who loved him. He had also begun his work in the nonprofit arena in a more structured way and was on the advisory boards of a few charities around Venice Beach and Santa Monica.

I had been building my career in the retail/fashion space and was working over sixty-hour weeks as an assistant buyer for a major retailer. We only had one car, a soft-top Jeep, and Merlin would drive me to work and pick me up in downtown Los Angeles—from and to our home in Venice. Anyone reading this in the L.A. area knows that traffic now would make this a no-go, yet years ago it worked. Merlin was working long hours too as his business grew, and he had not perfected the art of saying "no" to his clients.

Together, we were experiencing a trust and a freedom within our relationship that translated to supporting authentic growth along our individual paths as well. We were having fun and the independence-loving me was in a good space. We had talked about getting married, and it always came down to me saying, "Not yet" or "We are good right now." I did not really want to get married, as I felt that what we had worked. I just knew Merlin was my partner and we didn't need a cultural norm such as marriage to stamp it "Approved."

OK, SO EVERYTHING CAN CHANGE IN AN INSTANT

Life was full and we were tired, so we decided to take a trip to Kauai, in Hawaii, to be completely away from our work and enjoy being outside of our day-to-day routine. I knew that Kauai would be a good place to unwind. What I didn't know at the time was that Merlin was going to Kauai with a plan.

When we landed in Kauai and our luggage did not, my normally easy-going Merlin was acting all edgy and not his usual peaceful self at all. He did not want to leave the airport until we got our luggage. A hard stance. This isn't really the way it works when luggage is lost, and, besides, we were in Kauai—what did we really need but bathing suits we could easily purchase on the way to the hotel? I laughed at how out of character he was, and he was not happy about my lightness—he did not want to talk about it. He was visibly agitated. We ended up leaving the airport without our luggage, and Merlin literally paced and paced until it arrived later that night. Even after it arrived, Merlin was still not himself and did not want to talk to me about it.

In my head, I was thinking that I would go find a beach and be alone for a bit, to give Merlin space to process whatever he had going on. I wasn't aware of his needs, as I was so focused on catching up on sleep, sleep, and more sleep. I thought that's what he wanted too. That first night, Merlin did not sleep. He stayed up all night, waiting for the morning and me to wake up. Um, we were on vacation, so I was sleeping *in*.

When I finally opened my eyes, Merlin was right there, ready to talk to me about the hike to the waterfall he wanted to do. I was super committed to being on the beach and not moving all day. This was not what Merlin wanted to hear. I was in vacation mode and couldn't have been more relaxed. Merlin was in going-to-ask-me-to-marry-him mode and couldn't have been more stressed.

He came up with a compromise. I would hang on the beach alone for a few hours, and he would take a bike ride. At lunchtime, we would re-connect and head to the waterfall on the other side of the island. All good!

The ring Merlin made for me in a jewelry-making class (a very cool foreshadowing, as Dogeared was not even a thought yet) had lived many places during the previous thirty-six hours we had spent on the island—including in his luggage *(a single pearl of wisdom: Never put anything as precious as an engagement ring in your checked luggage)*. Ultimately, the ring ended up in the ceiling vent of our hotel room. He was so sure I was going to find it, even though I did not know that "it" existed.

As we hiked up to the waterfall in the misty rain, I was happy to be hugged by nature like this. Merlin was right about hiking. Mother Earth always gives, and I was grateful to receive. When Merlin got on one knee on the muddy hillside, with all the elements of nature being our witness, my answer came so easily . . .

"YES, YES, YES!!!"

With no effort, it was a big YES!

I'm not sure what shifted in me; I just knew that this was right. My inner hippie smiled, and my young woman's soul was ready to be Mrs. Clarke. Clarke with an "E." There was lots of kissing and hugging and laughing, and a fun re-hashing of what it took to get us to Kauai and on that hike. It was the start of the next chapter of *us*.

We encountered a guy smoking weed on our way down the trail, and Merlin told him excitedly, "Hey, we just got engaged!"

In a very drowsy, stoned voice, he responded: "Beautiful things happen in paradise, man."

Yes, they do.

Those words became the magic carpet ride of our marriage. Somehow, we knew that the paradise found in exquisite places like Kauai was alive inside us, and we were going to keep choosing *that*. And that knowing has only grown and strengthened over time.

When we got home from that trip, there was a huge banner across the front of our house that read, "Hey honey, will you marry me?" My sweet Merlin, always showing me the ways he loves. I remember thinking, *I am going to marry a man named Merlin. There is, for sure, magic ahead.*

Foreshadowing yet again.

A little sidenote of fun . . . I always thought I would be with someone with an accent. I was an International Studies major for while in college, as I wanted to learn about other cultures. I loved travel and beautiful, melodic languages, and the way the men I would meet pronounced my name (*Mahhhr•seé•ah* . . . imagine a Greek or Italian tone here). I am not sure an East Coast Bostonian accent was on the top of the pronunciation list, yet I am proud to be Merlin's *Maah ́•sha,* or just *Maah ́sh.* Marrying someone from Boston comes with automatic unconditional love for many sports teams and for the city itself. I was so ready to explore everything that an East Coast orientation offers. Especially the gorgeous trees and leaves during the fall—I can *feel* them. Fall beauty takes my breath away. I feel like I am experiencing God. I am a proud leaf peeper. Those colors are my church. Mother Nature is my BFF.

MERLIN + MARCIA + 2 MORE MAGICAL BEINGS = INFINITE LOVE

Me being a bit more cautious with things (like the really big things), I kept putting off having children. I was comfortable with Merlin + Marcia enjoying life—until one movie night where the popcorn was delicious, and the ending was even better. Merlin and I were watching *When a Man Loves a Woman* and up comes the scene where Andy Garcia is playing with his child. Merlin turned to me with tears in his eyes, saying, "It's time for us to have kids."

And so, it was.

That's how things have happened in our lives. Give us a good movie, some popcorn, a bit of raw emotion, and boom! We decide to have children.

OK, but now, how many?

For a while I thought I wanted four or five kids because someone once told me to imagine what you want your Thanksgiving table to look like. So, this number of children sounded like a good table to me. Two miscarriages and two children later and we were *in it,* barely keeping our heads above water. Catching our breath whenever we could. Laughing, crying, and sometimes both at the same time. Parenting is something that hits all parts of your heart and opens it up wider than anything imaginable.

News flash: Kids don't come with a user's manual, and it's a great deal of trial and error. We approached it all with love and a sense of humor. Humor! We are so lucky. We live with a lot of laughter in large part because Merlin is super funny. Our daughter Grace inherited this gift from him. Even today, I laugh out loud with him; it's one of my favorite things to do. I believe laughing cures so much. The release and reset of energy that a laugh brings make everything better. Tough parenting day. World-feels-off day. Yes, bring on the humor! It's such an important part of what makes us, us.

I think children helped us grow more than anything else. Our biggest conversations—the sideways ones and the easy ones—have been around our kids: their well-being, our well-being. I used to think that the goal for our kids was for them to be happy, yet a dear doctor I work with once told me that it's not only about happiness. It's also about purpose and ensuring that they are on a good path—a path that will reveal their purpose step by step in their own divine timing.

Merlin and I have always made decisions for Dogeared based on our desire to be good parents and live a life where we can be available for our children. As they were growing up, this meant that many times we walked away from big business deals, as we just didn't see how we could support them and be the parents we wanted to be. Time is the real gift. We wanted to have the time and space—to coach, to help in the classroom, to watch a recital, and to be the kind of house where other kids could come play and feel wholly welcomed. We were honored to have kids. We were committed to keeping our business smaller and manageable. It came down to managing resources and figuring out what was enough to live well. We were cultivating a personal nimbleness, a willingness to be in flow that I believe we all desire and deserve. We were so grateful and humbled to even be able to have this choice.

We thought after the kids turned eighteen that parenting life would ease up a bit. They would be "adults" and on their merry way. And of course, growth doesn't really happen in such a linear fashion. Even today, we still offer the compass of our love, and I believe our parenting is stronger now than it's ever been. We get to help our young adults shape lives that are on purpose and find the passion that keeps them turned on to the present moment, as well as future possibilities.

We are more flexible and open now, much more so than when they were younger. Maybe it's just us having more life experience and knowing with certainty that life's bumps and curves are inherent in the journey. Life will teach them. And, really, it's about the journey, right?

M + M as parents = gratitude squared.

PEARLS OF WISDOM

Merlin always says—life will teach them. I
think this means that we get to set some
guardrails and let the rest ride. Experiencing
life is the best teacher. No good or bad, just
a string of experiences that make up who
we are and how we navigate. It's all *for* us.

MY HUSBAND IS A BUS DRIVER

Through all our lows and highs, there have been energies play-ing together of love, peace, and joy, keeping us feeling safe and purposeful. Living a life where being in service is a daily conversation. What a powerful and beautiful way to live.

Merlin was always giving back in a grassroots way, and this gave him the structure to have bigger impact. He was my first lens into this type of work. And there was never a lot of talk about what he was going to do; he would just do it. He would see a need and do something kind. Kindness ruled.

I remember Robert, a veteran who was always hanging out at the ATM machine at our bank, which was just down the street from our house. Merlin would often talk to him and grew to understand his life and why he lived in the area out-side of the bank, unhoused. He was a man with a big story. Merlin would take Robert to eat at local restaurants, give him money, and try to get him housing, which Robert did not want. What mattered to Merlin was that Robert, who was reg-ularly unseen, could feel seen, heard, and cared for.

Speaking of banks, there was also Frances, the bank robber who was newly out of jail. Merlin met him through a friend.

Frances had used his finger in his jacket to look like a gun, his only weapon, to hold up five banks. He spent twelve years in jail. In his heart, he was not a bank robber, rather an addict feeding his addiction. Merlin gave him odd jobs, even though we didn't really have any odd jobs to give. He was just supporting a man whose life had not been kind to him.

The list of people we have met and connected with through Merlin's commitment to kindness and connection is one of my favorite parts of who we are. We would go camping and he would leave jewelry on cards in the trees or on trails for people to find. A surprise. Sprinkling kindness wherever he went.

For his mom's ninetieth birthday, Merlin's gift to her was to give away a piece of Dogeared jewelry every day in her honor. 365 days of giving. He made up a card with her cute face on it and told the story of the gift—of celebrating Ann. Every recipient would understand this was a simple act of love in motion. We knew that each piece of jewelry ended up where it needed to be and who it needed to be with. The jewelry always found them. Merlin was creative in how he gave these away, putting them in random places like bike baskets, shopping carts, and nooks and crannies all over the globe. Far and wide, people were receiving some Dogeared/Ann love.

Ann passed away that year, and Merlin kept giving the jewelry away. Sometimes he would sit near the place where he had left one of the gifts to see the reaction of the people finding the jewels. He loved doing this. He smiled as he watched, and we know Ann did too. Such a good son. Through his actions, he has taught me how to give and be in service, as it is in his soul to do so. He grabbed this part of his soul's passion early on and just ran with it.

Maybe it's the soul's passion that also makes us curious. Merlin, while a creature of habit in some ways, is one of the most curious humans I know. His curiosity keeps us both in a youthful state, as he meets new people daily and is always learning and growing. Nothing is linear with him, even his habits. I still, after all these years, do not know exactly what will stick and what will move on. Yes, some foundational concepts are solid, and integrity and service are at the basis of everything he does. And as he discovers and lives his life in a grand way, his life experiences truly influence him. This leads to new openings, artistic pathways, and even career changes. He is always creating.

Anything is possible. He could tell me today that he wants to buy a 1971 Volkswagen (VW) bus and become a bus driver. He could tell me that he wants to go out into the world on this bus and connect people, organizations, and communities in their goals to heal and to love themselves and each other. He could say he wants to do this through conversation *and* action—to do good by supporting people in the ways they really want support. He could tell me all this, and I would be excited for him, and excited for us.

And not long ago, he did just that. The Healing Bus is represented by that VW bus. When people ask Merlin what he does, he sometimes responds with, "I am a bus driver." After thirty years of working within Dogeared, Merlin is now driving a vehicle of change and transformation. He has been the guy within our Dogeared domain to manage our giving and community outreach, and now this is becoming what he does full time. The Healing Bus—a social enterprise committed to bringing healing to communities in need—is his biggest focus right now.

The magic carpet rides again (this time disguised as a bus)!

CHAPTER 3

SMALL "d" BECOMES A BIG "D"

Working in the corporate fashion world in the late eighties as a buyer for a major department store was a dream job. I was happy, busy, and being mentored by some of the best in the business. It was a good fit for me and gave me much of the background and training I would eventually use for Dogeared, although at the time there was no Dogeared even being dreamed of.

I started making jewelry as a form of creative expression. My side hustle. If your mind is anything like mine, it goes *all day long*. And I discovered that making things with my hands and my heart was a soothing salve for my mind. It was the mixture of relief and fun that I needed.

I had no formal training in jewelry making and have never even considered myself a crafty person. Sitting on our bed at night, Merlin used to take out an electric drill and drill holes for me, bead by bead, so the sewing needles I was using to

36

string beads would fit through. We did not know there were such useful tools as beading needles that are fine as hair, strong like wire, and that fit through many beads. Labor costs were cut by 90 percent with one amazing needle. "There's nothing like the right tool for the right job," Merlin would often repeat like a mantra as he drilled away.

PEARLS OF WISDOM

There's nothing like the right
tool for the right job.
Efficiency and effectiveness = game-changer!

A friend of mine joined us in this exploration. She and I were both in the same place, feeling like we wanted to have some creative fun and see if we could sell anything we made. We would set up our booth at the Pasadena Rose Bowl flea market, Ugg boots on and hot tea in hand, as it was icy cold at 5:00 a.m. We made pens with flowers on the ends of them, beaded chains for eyeglasses, and other useful and non-useful items that we just felt like making. My friend's mom even made potpourri bean bag frogs that sold out every time—her nod to Beanie Babies. At the time, we had no set pricing, no style numbers, and no brand name. But we did have some serious satisfaction. This kind of selling—selling what we had created from love and a place of free expression—was super soul-filling. There were no rules. There was no pressure.

On the porch in our bikinis, having some margaritas, my friend and I combed a thesaurus to figure out the name of our business. My friend loved animals, so when the word "dogeared" popped up, it just felt right. We both liked the animal reference that wasn't really an animal reference. We have all folded down pages of a book, a magazine, or a journal. We "dogear" things that are personally meaningful and that we want to return to again and again. This was a beautiful intersection for us.

After many years of doing the job that I loved as a buyer, I was recruited by a big brand at the time, Esprit, to help in sales for a new division they were creating. I had not done sales at this level, but I believe they hired me for my buyer background—so I could talk the talk and walk the walk with the buyers that would come through the door to buy this new line. I quickly realized, however, that sales was totally not my thing. There is a personality trait that I believe a good sales-person has, and that trait was missing from my DNA. A com-petitiveness that just wasn't there for me. When the division closed and I was laid off, I remember calling Merlin—needing his calm in my storm. He quickly reminded me that I really did not love selling, or the job. *Oh, yeah!* I think I was shocked at being laid off at such a young age. At the time, I thought that only happened to people much older than me. I'm not sure why I associated age and being laid off together, but I did.

Merlin and I decided that I would take a break and sim-ply be peaceful for a bit. He was doing well enough with his graphic design business to keep us going. I had worked long hours for many years, so a break sounded sort of divine. I em-barked on some fun lunching and day drinking, sleeping in, and doing life with no clock governing it. It felt like a really nice vacation, a much-needed recharge. After just a few weeks, I had a feeling, a push—an energy that was both external and internal that it was time for something different. A different rhythm, a new clock. I get these inner promptings in my life sometimes. I think we all do. And when I listen and act on these angelic taps on my shoulder, and trust in them, I am usually surprised about the journey forward.

THE SIDE HUSTLE TAKES CENTER STAGE

With my side hustle creativity flourishing, surprises were beginning to pop. My friend and I found we had a product that would sell out each time we made it. It was a line of fabric chokers with charms hanging from them. Since we both had retail backgrounds, we thought about selling these to stores to see what would happen. I had a friend who was working as a jewelry buyer for a major department store. I called her and asked if she would look at our line of chokers, mostly for feedback on the direction we were taking. That conversation turned into our first big department store order. I felt pure elation when she said she wanted to buy it to test in ten stores. My ego was getting some love. But more interestingly, I sensed that good universal timing was at play! This time of transition really deepened my trust in that timing, as it always comes through whether we realize it at the time or not.

Once we took that order, the flood gates opened. The side hustle became the main event. We were doing Dogeared full-time. We were a real company. We had ship dates and accounting and all things that companies have. When we cut 400 chokers an inch too small, we cried, and then we cut another 400 chokers the right length. When we could not get the supplies we wanted, we got the supplies we needed. It was real, and exciting, and day and night. One of our vendors lived a few streets away, so he would drop off paper bags of gems and supplies—and we would smile, imagining what our neighbors probably thought. It was fun. It was stressful. It was the beginning. The beginning of *what* we were not sure, but it made us happy, and it was ours.

———————— ✦ ————————

We were always up late the night before a trade show, and one summer night in August, Merlin and I were *in it!* When I am up against a deadline, I am in my zone, as I have usually procrastinated, which puts me in this situation more times than not.

At about 2:00 a.m. I had made a tiny wishbone necklace on a colorful silk string, and I wanted to attach it to a card with some messaging, as it would display better at the stores. The concept for the card came through earlier in the week when I was reading a story on the power of believing and the power of intention. This resonated with me, and I thought the concept would create more good energy with our jewelry. The message that came through me for the wishbone was this:

Paired with this message, it was a piece that had a punch—*we were selling something that we were telling you would break.* And break for a good reason! This was great for us as a business: no returns! Simplicity at its finest. But more importantly, I loved the idea that when you were buying this piece for the way it looked, you would also get a secondary gift: the message on a card that would empower you. At the time, jewelry was not displayed this way, and this "Make a Wish" necklace would be our tester. The card concept would become what we were known for and how we would disrupt a marketplace.

Merlin lives by the creed "happy wife, happy life," so in those wee hours of the morning, he very kindly created the card that we would take to the show. He designed it so the necklace would wrap around the card twice (being a good length for someone to wear), and the charm would hang nicely in the front of the card. That is how we chose the size of the card and the jewelry. Quick yet thoughtful decisions as we got ready for the show in the middle of the night.

PEARLS OF WISDOM

Happy wife, happy life.
Self-explanatory, right?

MESSAGES, MEANING, AND CONNECTION

In 2003, we sold our first carded piece of jewelry. Our business had been in play, and we were making uncarded beautiful jewels, and the message/card with the jewelry changed our business forever. Fast-forward over twenty years, and that beautiful white 4x4 card with simple messaging both launched and has sustained our global business. The size of the card and the messaging became synonymous with all things Dogeared. We were trusting in the power of people's own intentions and connection to their own abilities to use Dogeared as a reminder to source their dreams and believe in themselves. I would always laugh when my friends would come up to me and let me know that it had been a year and the Make a Wish silk necklace was still around their neck. "Not ready yet," I would gently say, as I also believe in divine timing, a concept that no one wants to discuss when they are ready for things to happen now! We heard hundreds of stories of our Make a Wish necklaces doing their thing—breaking in a most affirming way for the wearer. We would smile when we received an occasional return of a broken one with a request for either a credit or a new necklace. We were always happy to oblige.

From the beginning, our jewels were representative of a power to believe in oneself to *create*—to create change, healing, babies, boyfriends, girlfriends, spouses, inner peace, and success of all kinds. They were reminders of celebrations and touch stones for connection—connection to lost loved ones and to all of life's experiences. The power was in the simplicity of believing in the message.

We sold tens of thousands of these necklaces. The Make a Wish product line has lots of colors of silk, lots of different charms and gems, and lots of different messages that always ended in the phrase, "When your necklace wears off, your wish is ready to come true." We had created a catalyst on a global scale and having this kind of impact was so exciting. The Dogeared energy is one of love, healing, connection, and authenticity. This energy would become foundational to all the products we created from this point on. The messaging on our cards and the pieces of jewelry were external reminders of internal feelings. When you put your Dogeared on, it was the convergence of feminine energies: of inner wisdom, peace, knowing, and empathy, all connecting with the external world. It was about the person putting it on. A connection with something complete and whole. A connection with something outside and inside of yourself that soothed or confirmed. A channel to wisdom that was not completely apparent in a physical realm. Call it divine guidance or talking to your angels; call it your connection with God, or yourself, or to something wise and otherworldly. This was the bond. And a powerful one it was. Your own little power center. A place that was meaningful to you, the wearer.

For many years, we operated like this, making jewelry that we wanted to wear ourselves. We participated in countless tradeshows and won awards for booth design. One time, we created a forest with flame-retardant green velvet walls and branches that displayed our jewels. We hired our first sales rep, whose expertise was selling to small specialty stores.

After some time, my friend-turned-business-partner decided to go in a different direction, and Merlin and I took on Dogeared ourselves. Merlin in a part-time, being-a-good-husband kind of way, and me as a full-time, real-life, "Oh my God, I am going to do this!" kind of way.

In those first days of our Dogeared journey, when we chose our brand name with the help of a little tequila and a lot of laughter, the word "dogeared" popped up from the page of that thesaurus in lowercase letters. But eventually the small "d" became a capital "D"—as this business was born and grew into itself. It was the transition of a word to a living, breathing energy. We chose our name from a place of true freedom. No thought to marketing, longevity, or even if the name truly described the jewelry we were selling. We did not start Dogeared with a solid foundation or intricate blueprint, just a knowing that we wanted *to create something* that supported our need *to do something*. No formal business plans, or investors, or even a thought about the month or year ahead.

We leaned into Nike's tag line, "Just do it!"

CHAPTER 4

MONEY IS ENERGY ... AND SOMETIMES IT MAKES ME MOODY

The word "abundance" is a part of my everyday language. It's like an old, dear friend who hangs out with me all day. A presence, not just a word. It can show up as living with an "and" mindset. Recently, a friend of mine and I planned a walk. When I asked her if we were walking the dogs or walking the beach with just us, she said she would like to do both. (Dog walks are shorter, as our dogs don't like to go as far as we do!) I said, YES! It's an "I get to," not an "I have to" way to move through life. Freedom to choose to take two walks or to rest all day, that is also abundance. The allowance of time, the freedom to choose, and the mindset to experience and be curious. It's living in abundance. I enjoy amplifying the energy of it in simple ways, like wearing abundance essential oils and diffusing them throughout my home.

More deeply, abundance shows up within the interconnecting circle of love that is my family and friends. Big love that I work toward and for. I live abundantly in thought and in feeling (most of the time), and I aim to meet all my life this way.

Even though I know that all of this serves me, and I make this my practice, I still get caught. My mind . . . oh, my mind.

ME + MERLIN — M SQUARED IN ACTION

Before kids, before Dogeared, there were few responsibilities except to each other, and of course the essentials like rent, food, and fun. Merlin was making good money as a graphic designer, and I was working in retail, not making great money. But between the two of us, we were making it work, living in Venice, California, and enjoying the freedom of just us. Money wasn't something that we discussed a lot, as our basic needs were met, and we were living with an attitude of simplicity around money. Working hard, loving what we were doing, we were in an attitude of *yes*. Vacation next week—let's do it! Dinner at the new restaurant down the street—*yes!* Between credit cards and our bank account, there was an ease and quickness to our decision-making around all things "just us." Freedom of mind and spirit. A powerful and peaceful place to reside.

When the Dogeared journey started, we did not give thought to anything except a new beginning, some creative inspiration, and the reality that we got to make stuff. As a dear friend of mine says, "Making stuff is fun!"

This was a time when sales and cash flow were not even something we discussed, so when we needed things for the business, we would simply look at which credit card could handle a charge and buy it—charging this card, looking at when that one was due, and finding cards that had zero percent interest for a period of time so that we could buy inventory. Can you hear the music cue? Because this was when the money dance was in the house. *Oh, yeah.* The ease of choice around money had a distinct groove to it.

We started Dogeared with some credit and a little bit of cash. It was a game we were playing with money, and we had no fear of anything financial. We had no responsibility to anyone, except us. It was all very clear. We were starting a business, and we were trusting ourselves and that universal connection that we believed guided us to this place. Not oriented around the future, we were highly present, adventurous, and following all the signs, signals, and opportunities that were right in front of us.

At the time I didn't understand what a beautiful gift it was to live in this presence—this presence that I talk about in many aspects of my world. But I do now. This presence *and* this financial presence. A powerful combo. I believe this set a blueprint for the lifelong journey that Dogeared has become.

WITH ABUNDANCE COMES RESPONSIBILITY—THE BIG LEARNING

When Dogeared was more established, and we were doing it for "real"—meaning we had people who helped manage the money and people who were relying on us, either our team or our customers—once a week, I would light a candle, grab a glass of wine, and go over the weekly financial reporting that our accounting team had sent to me. This is a good life habit that I'm still committed to—*pairing something I am not excited about with something I am.* (Cabernet and laundry, anyone?)

With wine glass in hand, I would put a check mark next to every deposit made and check written, and I'd question anything not in sequence. It was my elementary way of understanding the money coming in and the money going out. A key element to any business. I also signed every check written. In addition to the weekly overall financial report, I would get daily deposit reporting. It was finance 101, and it worked for me. Money was both my nemesis and my love child, as I was responsible for the optimal timing of the money dance.

The bottom line is that no one is accountable to and for your money like you are. No one. A lesson Merlin and I would learn on repeat. (See the next chapters for a couple of memorable *WTF?* stories that may inspire you toward greater accountability too.)

Being an entrepreneur is a 24/7 gig, so managing all of Dogeared in this way, with these practices as our foundation, allowed us to sleep at night. Merlin and I decided what our finances did or did not do. That's how being responsible gave us a place to rest, even in the midst of our growth and expansion.

THE SLIDE FROM PLENTY TO NOT ENOUGH

In my head, there was so much freedom to having cash in the bank and a constant current of it coming in. Then the inverse would pop into my head. I would feel the not-enough story asserting itself . . . *I am not enough to maintain this. I have no clue what I am doing. There is not enough in the bank for everything we are working on. It's going to run out soon.* I would not trust. Worry and fear would seep into my spirit and visit me for a bit. Yep, with abundance comes responsibility, which translated to a bigness—a "Hey, it's really real"-ness as people were relying on us.

When you are caring for yourself, your own family, and the many families of those who work with you, that freedom that I love about being an entrepreneur can feel not-so-free. Our team worked with us so they could pay their bills, feed their kids, and meet other needs that come along with living a nice life. Every decision I made, and every decision my immediate team made, had direct impact on the hundreds of people who were relying on us to do well by the company and by them. When you have other people's livelihoods in your hands, you want good, strong calloused hands steering the ship. Experienced hands that aren't making big, huge mistakes—and that can quickly course-correct when small mistakes happen. Our callouses were thickening each day and were earned with the experience and practice we were gaining by the minute. Many times, this included Merlin and I not taking a paycheck to make sure that the money needed was there for everyone else. Not my favorite steps in the choreography of the money dance.

When we were putting money into Dogeared from our savings, credit cards, borrowing from all kinds of places, and not taking a paycheck, I was moody—not happy, not in the whirl of the life I loved living. My moodiness would emerge in a variety of ways. My thinking would become small, no dreaming allowed. Everything seemed impossible. I would not sleep well. It was a big haze over my world.

Most of the time when I was in this non-trusting place, I would go internal—not communicating how I was feeling to Merlin, as I did not want him to worry about me or the money. I was not in a place to let in the beautiful stories of connection and love that we were hearing on the daily from our Dogeared customers. I would temporarily let my perception of our money become the primary marker of success. From every kind of perspective and practice that I believe in, I know that is just not so, yet my mind said it was so.

Money is a currency, an energetic tide, and there are many currencies that I believe in my heart are so much more accessible when your fundamental financial needs are met. Making decisions solely from a financial perspective—without looking through another lens, like love—just did not feel integrated or good. My mind was bumping into my heart, which just did not work with how we were typically operating in our world. Most of the time, we were working with the heart-centered currencies of love, family, commitment, health, friendship, kindness, community . . . the list is a long one. We were exchanging positive vibes that create all things positive—an exciting stream of cash, creative ideas, vibrant energy, warm feelings, and more. When I moved out of the way of my mind, communicated with Merlin, and focused on the other currencies, cash would be there. New opportunities came knocking, like licensing deals with the producers of blockbuster movies. These partnerships created lots of excitement in all realms—including the money I stressed over to run our business, as these deals required a great deal of money to make them successful. Such a paradox, right?

I like living in a space where I am not concerned about making payroll, paying our vendors, and paying ourselves. You may understand this divide very well, as I believe money conversations show up for everyone at some time in their life. Most of our team had no idea what that responsibility felt like or looked like, as their commitment was to show up and do the work they were hired to do, and not to worry about the financial operations of the company.

THE CHA-CHA-CHA OF PROBLEMS AND SOLUTIONS

When we knew that Dogeared had a real future—when it was clear to us that its beautiful energy wanted to consolidate and really be here—finances became something that we discussed on the regular. We discovered that more consistent conversations brought more comfort and ease. Having a routine that we could rely upon was distinctly calming. Having CFOs, accounting managers, accounts payable specialists, accounts receivable specialists, controllers, and other humans who love managing all-things money did not mean I could leave this dance to someone else. It meant that my role could *grow*. I could expand my awareness of what I needed to do and could do beyond using my #2 Ticonderoga pencil.

Yes, I love #2 pencils, but it was a time for expansion, and we were being shown another way. I was expanding my tool belt and pushing outside of what was comfortable for me. We had large credit lines from banks, we had good balances in our accounts, and most of the time, Merlin and I were getting a paycheck too. I am a Sagittarius, which means that freedom-seeking is part of my DNA. Many entrepreneurs want the same (no matter what their astrological chart looks like). I was coming to understand just how beautifully communication, a positive mindset, and some action (especially around money) can support goals and intentions—and vice versa. I was able to see money as a motivator, mostly as a means to something I wanted to experience. If you tend to procrastinate, like I do, money can be a fuel to ignite us in to action.

By the way, managing this part of the business didn't demand a lot of time from us. For me, it represented maybe a few hours each week. Powerful hours that set in motion some of our biggest opportunities to learn. There is a spiritual aspect to money that we were both ripe to explore—and so we did.

. . . .

PEARLS OF WISDOM

Good sales can fix many things.
Always focus on the sales, which means
always focus on your customers. I typically
do not love "absolute" terminology, yet it's
appropriate here. Know your customers.
Understand who they are, what they like,
how they want to see you, and how you
can solve specific problems for them.
A great sales team, strong management, and
products that customers love did this for us.

. . . .

At important stages of Dogeared's growth, each of those money-savvy people listed previously would give me options for calculated risks on decisions that would impact the business. *Do we open a store? Do we hire internally and run our own warehouse? Do we offer unlimited vacation? Do we provide display units to our retailers? Do we create a customer loyalty program? Do we become a B Corporation? Do we do the Dr. Maya Angelou licensing deal. (Um, this one was an easy YES!)* This was the good stuff. The fun stuff. Making decisions and seeing how they truly played out.

We always appreciated the team members who brought to our attention what we could do better, as they often came with solutions to the issues at hand—which then became opportunities to grow and change. I learned in my time working with the big retailers to always bring a solution. Being a solver shows creativity, and it shows that you are a team player and someone people want to invest in. Issues are aplenty in business, so I recommend being the one who helps by bringing the energy to solve. Good wisdom for all of life, really.

PEARLS OF WISDOM

Say it with me now:
I always bring solutions!

I grew up at Dogeared, in all ways. As a business owner, mom, friend, wife, creator, and woman. Just like the gems we use in our pieces, there were many facets to navigate—the intersecting aspects of business, life, and an evolving self. A healthy relationship with all things financial also being one of those facets. I learned and grew as the money path opened, closed, shifted, turned, U-turned, and about-faced. Giving my power and my moods over to money was something that I would explore throughout many years as an entrepreneur. Even when there is clearly enough money, I can still go to lack. If I look at my various life and money eras, especially those with responsibility attached to them, I see a pattern—when I had the most money, I thought about money; when I had the least amount, I thought about money. I know it's just part of my personal growth—an invitation to just flat out believe that I am cared for and have always been cared for. Tending to this energy is part of the dance of running Dogeared, and I get to remind myself that I *love* to dance.

It starts with me. It's the circulation of wealth, health, and affirming thoughts—actions and words that create. The universe "hears" me and "sees" me. Calculated risk + divine intervention + the universal law of attraction—attracting back to you what you put out into the world through your thoughts, actions, and feelings.

• •

PEARLS OF WISDOM

Trust in your vision.
Believe in yourself.
Take small actions.
Don't attach to outcome, as it can be limiting.
Stay present.
Enjoy your journey!
And . . . be open to some divine
and universal support.

• •

HEY, WE DID BECOME A B CORPORATION!

About those calculated risks mentioned above . . .

Eventually Merlin found the B Corporation (B Corp) community, which offered solid guidelines for us as we were strengthening the foundation of our business. It provided guardrails for us to grow within and to be accountable to. The values of being a B Corporation (benefit corporation) resonated with us, each based on having a positive impact on employees, the community, society, and the environment. It gave us the framework and confidence to make good decisions that were not only best for the business, but also best for our team and the wider world.

The first B Corp application was about ninety pages long, and I remember telling Merlin that we didn't have the bandwidth to take this on. Merlin believed in what they were offering and put in the work with some of our team. Before the certification assessment, we felt we were doing a pretty good job. Taking the assessment, we realized we could do a lot better. One of the areas that it catalyzed was offering paid volunteer days. This way, our team members got to connect with their favorite communities and be purposeful at places like the Downtown Women's Center, Step Up Women's Network, Lipstick Angels, and others.

In all, the certification process cost over $100,000, and it took a year to implement the changes to how we were running things. We officially became a B Corporation in 2011. We were one of the first jewelry companies to become one. We are in good company, as big players like Patagonia and Ben & Jerry's are B Corps. We wanted our consumers to know that purchasing from Dogeared was purchasing from a company that is working daily to be better. Every few years we need to be recertified, which allows us the opportunity to see where we have succeeded and where we can do better. It comes back to that foundational knowing—that being the kind of company we want to be is a journey, not a destination.

CHAPTER 5

"I AM NOT STEALING AS MUCH AS EVERYONE ELSE!"

Since its first days, Dogeared has been a living canvas for creating beauty. As we went about the business of designing jewelry and the messaging that gave extra love to our jewels, we also created a beautiful culture within our Dogeared walls. We hired families, mothers, sisters, sons, daughters, husbands, cousins, and family friends. We loved having family dynasties in our space. We had a homelike feeling in our workspace, and as a result, people worked for us for a long time. We saw potential in people and gave them opportunities to grow. We had internal committees, like the Do-Good Team (customer service), the Hiring Gems Team (recruiting), and the Be Balanced Team (wellness). Each team supported the well-being of all. It was a positive place to be and team members enjoyed the work and being with each other.

We provided educational opportunities, we helped with funeral arrangements, we bought cars and refrigerators, and sponsored little league teams. We had a bowling team, parties at the park with food trucks, big holiday gatherings, and the celebration of more milestone moments than I can recall.

One of my favorite memories of us all being together happened on one of my birthdays. The exec team hired a guitarist with an amplifier to come into our studio and sing Ray LaMontagne's "You Are the Best Thing"—one of my favorite songs. Months earlier, I had shared with our management team that I had taken guitar lessons, as I wanted to play the song for Merlin for his birthday. I told them how hard it was to play, and how I had not mastered it, or even gotten past the first "You are the best thing." Now here we were on my birthday, more than one hundred of us, listening to this musician play this song with ease and grit. We swayed and danced together. Music and dancing for me are always a soul place, as you've likely surmised by now. It was the perfect gift.

PEARLS OF WISDOM

To me, *an experience* is the best
gift you can give or receive.

Merlin and I were committed to being there in all ways for our team. We had an emergency fund that was almost always a "yes" to whoever was asking for financial help. We created a profit sharing plan, so when we had a good year, we could share the success with the people who had worked so hard to get us there. All of it was an evolution as we figured out, daily, how to make good decisions for the business, our team, and ourselves. How to physically interact with each other with kindness and respect. And how to do this all under the umbrella of the care and feeding of the business and the global community we had the privilege of being part of. Before becoming a B Corporation, we had no blueprint besides intuition, love, and knowing who we were and who we wanted to be as a brand.

We worked with small vendors who we had very close relationships with and helped them grow their businesses as we were growing ours. We gave Dogeared jewelry and money to many nonprofits to support their efforts, and for many years we kept it private, as that was what we felt was appropriate.

We were a family. There was depth and realness with our Dogeared community that we experienced every day. This connectedness was always something we were excited about, and we were always striving to show up as big as we could. At one point, we even investigated buying an apartment building so we could provide well-priced housing for our team in the very expensive Los Angeles area.

PEARLS OF WISDOM

Being entrepreneurs, many of us learn as we go. When the good is good, congratulations to you! When the big opportunities arise for learning, congratulations to you! You just do your best to make good decisions for yourself, your team, and your business.

Our commitment was having real-life results. We were sold in thousands of stores across the globe. You could find our jewels in thirty-seven countries. We were in just about every major department store, both in-store and online. Our pieces were in movies, TV, and in the hands of Hollywood stylists daily. We had negotiated super-fun licensing deals for big movies like *Eat Pray Love* and *Sex and the City*. We were *soooo* happy when we were awarded the licensing opportunity for Dr. Maya Angelou through her family foundation. Her poetry, our jewels = career dream coming true. We were the mapmakers in our space, bringing to market everyday jewelry with simple, inspiring messaging.

———◆———

Happy thoughts. Focusing on all things positive. Good vibes only! This is how we wanted to live at home and at work. We were proud of our company culture and our community. And in a world of duality—where day meets night, where summer meets winter—it may have been inevitable that we would have to integrate the shadow side of all that light.

Many businesses go through some "not so bright" experiences, the likes of which many business owners don't discuss outside of their private circles. This stuff happens, no matter how much you don't want it to. Creativity spinning the wrong way.

Dogeared was not immune. As with all the stories in this book, this is my version, included here to show this side of business and our growth from it. Situations have been merged, names have been changed, and the threads of my truth are woven throughout.

Here we go . . .

We had a purchasing agent who had a spending addiction and charged his kids' swimming lessons and more on our corporate card. He also over-ordered by the thousands from just about every small and large vendor we had, putting us in a financial whirlwind of hurt, not to mention capsizing many of these vendors, as most were smaller businesses. He was recommended by someone who was working for us, and we were encouraged to hire him right away. Yes, we had internal checks and balances that should have caught all of this before it started, but obviously there was room to learn here.

We had another team member engage in time theft, meaning that someone else would clock them in when they were not there, or they would leave early and not clock out, and then say they had been there a full day.

We had someone running their own business on a website with stolen merchandise from our returns area. They flat-out lied and led us down a path of thinking it was someone else at first.

We navigated mental illness, drug addiction, and just about everything else that life throws at a family. We had a hard time delineating between business and personal and when and where to draw the line.

While all of this was happening behind the scenes, we were working to run the business and show up intentionally and purposefully for the majority of our team who worked so beautifully for Dogeared. So many of them still get together to this day, as long-lasting friendships, business relationships, and more were born from working on our team. I still see many of them too. We were like entertainers chanting the mantra "the show must go on!" We just wanted to take a deep breath and relax, and trust again, rather than navigate anything that was not perceived as a positive for us or the business.

Typically, when these situations came to light, we would create payment plans for people to pay us back, or we would give them another shot. Sometimes, and only sometimes, we would fire people. At the time, you had to work pretty hard to get fired, as we just didn't want to do it. Hindsight being what we all know it is, this was probably not the most accountable or sustainable approach. We worked to keep our focus on all the good things that were happening, and we chose not to dwell on missteps—and the side of humanity we were being shown, which of course exists but we did not like to acknowledge.

As in any business, when we did need to let someone go, it was not an easy process. In a weird way, sometimes the person being let go did not understand; they were in disbelief that we were acting like a business. I believe it was because so many aspects of their lives were intertwined with the company. Their friends and family were here, their social lives, and the business was personal to them, as it was to us. We had created safety, and just like within a family, people were given second and even third chances to remain in the "Dogeared Hug." This was the core of what all of us loved doing and being part of. Saying "so long" was very emotional for all of us, especially when it came with a big shot of betrayal.

Betrayal is a devastating energy. A storm of internal thunder that beats down on all parts of your body and soul, it lingers, deep and hard. Without invitation, it takes a seat in your daily routine, keeping itself alive like a screaming child who wants to make its presence *really* known.

Betrayal has the power to elevate itself over any kind of good, positive, or loving internal conversation. For me, during this period, it worked its way to the front of the line to be the dominant character in the book of "me" and just mixed itself into all my self-limiting beliefs—which, oddly, I am sure led to this vein of learning that kept the betrayal circle flowing. It was an in-your-face all the time kind of learning, as some of our trusted team members not only stole money and jewelry, but intangibles as well. From Merlin and me, they stole a good night's sleep, a peaceful Sunday, or a sense of confidence in what we were doing. "You've got this" was a wobbly statement during this chapter.

I would just store them away. The betrayals. I don't believe that human nature likes to take from others, so for me it was easiest to take my magic eraser and just wipe away the evidence that something had gone down. Erase the action, erase the hurt, erase the feelings, erase the betrayal. These experiences would go into the emotional shoebox sitting on the top shelf of my psyche, gathering energetic dust, sitting dormant until the energy could no longer be contained or kept quiet.

Magic erasers are amazing and wonderful tools, until they are not. If you don't want to see "it," "it" will keep showing up in all kinds of creative ways until your view is so chaotic and cluttered that you can't see what is right in front of you anymore. It's like driving down the foggiest, rainiest road with zero visibility, and fear is sitting right there in the front seat with you.

PEARLS OF WISDOM

It is important to note that not choosing to spend time seeing what is in front of you is a betrayal of yourself. You must spend time on clearing your lenses and looking with honesty at how to do "it" differently. In short, if I don't take care of me, I can't take care of you. And if I can't do that, then the world doesn't get my best self. And if the world doesn't get my best self . . . well, downward it goes.

The tipping point to all of this happened with someone we truly loved who had been with us for a long time. She had stolen over $150,000 over the course of a few years—doing it quietly, while we hugged her kids when they would come to visit our offices. Her family would join in to support nonprofit events we were doing. She had borrowed money from us and been given money from the emergency fund on numerous occasions—we always said "yes." She is someone I would have been sure would be with us still today.

When the truth came out, the reasons why were numerous, and all assigned to real-life situations that we could understand. But the actual stealing still gives me a catch in my breath when it darts into my mind loop every now and again, and I see her smile. Someone we knew so well stealing from us like this didn't seem possible—until it was. People taking from a company where there is no connection, where it's "just a job"—although not good of course—makes more sense. I imagine they see a company that has no face. But someone working side by side with Merlin and me, someone I cared for taking from us at this level was just something outside of my understanding.

This betrayal was different than the others. We needed an energetic shift, and for the universe to hear us loudly, clearly, and supportively.

Noooooooo More!!!!!!!!!! (Pro tip: Need a change? Yell this as loud as you can to an empty space! Very therapeutic.)

By ignoring and moving on and not having anyone be truly accountable for their actions, we were perpetuating a circle of ick that said to the universe, "Hey, steal from us! We are *not* going to do anything about it." I felt bad for them. I had so much empathy for someone feeling compelled to do something so wrong. These were good people making bad decisions.

The storyline that kept jumping in my face was an opportunity for all of us to grow. If they were not held accountable for their actions, where is the lesson in there for them? Me doing nothing did not serve either of our learnings or growth. It was hard, but I came to recognize that the school of life was in full session! It was time for personal accountability all the way around, including me taking responsibility for my part in what we were experiencing.

PEARLS OF WISDOM

If you always do what you have
always done, you will always get
what you have always gotten.
Meaning:
*If you want to change things in your life,
consider changing your own behavior. These
can be small shifts that make big impact.
Change your inner world, and your outer
world can't help but change too.*

The experiential 2x4s that kept hitting us over the head needed a rest. We had been heavily bruised. And just because I did not want to spend time on this mess did not mean that I could put my head in the sand. No more sand. Avoidance was super unfair to the team that was working so hard for our shared vision and the beauty we got to put into the world. Keeping my eye on that truth helped me to see that one of the most loving things I can ever do is to allow each person's journey to be what they make of it. How they live their life is their sacred choice. For me, this gave new meaning to the term "good vibes"—spreading positive thoughts, feelings, and energy in the most personally accountable way ever.

I was fully ready and willing to hold myself and everyone involved accountable . . .

Cue police with badges showing up to the offices.

Cue insurance companies and forensic accounting.

Cue detectives and the legal system.

Cue a jail sentence that is determined by the restitution paid back.

OK, so this was nowhere I wanted to spend any energy, but I did it. I did it with trust in my angels, myself, my Merlin, and the universe—all coming to my aid to help me truly understand that this course of action was *for* her—not against her. It was for her benefit as much as it was for me and Dogeared.

A lot of resources went into this process from our end. She did not admit anything at the beginning except an extra accidental check. We were growing too fast and did not have some of the systems we needed in the places we needed them, things like double signatures on checks or even a daily review by the manager with the accounting team of all transactions.

This case still goes on today, as many circumstances held up the sentencing process. Small things like a jammed legal system, a non-violent offense, a global reset (aka pandemic), and more. After we found out about the big steal, I never saw her again. Merlin and our team managed the hearings, insurance audits, and anything requiring a physical presence. This was self-care for me. Allowing others to do what needed to be done and trusting that what needed to be, would be.

———◆———

Another one of our big learning moments came for a different team member, one who yelled, "I am not stealing as much as everyone else!" in the middle of a private conversation we were having with him. This outburst happened as we were letting him go for an array of behaviors that just weren't cool, and we just wanted to understand the why. We had worked together for such a long time. We loved this person. What had shifted? What made him think it was a good idea to do this, and what made him do this to our business and to the rest of the team? What made him think it was OK? So many questions, and to my true sadness, he walked out of the office after saying it, leaving us to our own "mind-fun" (imagine the stories my mind created) and to manage the team that was unnerved by all of it.

When there are human resource issues, legally, there is very little we can share with anyone, so we had to trust that the team would trust that we were doing the best for them and the business. A big trust train.

PEARLS OF WISDOM

We took the approach of "trust, but verify."
In its simplest form it translates to, "I
believe you, *and* I need to see the receipt."
The trusting part is in my soul. Easy.
The verify part is the kicker.

The universe did shift as we shifted. We became solid in our knowing that things like this would not happen again. We were now fully awake and accountable to Ms. Dogeared and the many *amazing* people on our team who supported her journey and ours. That was our true responsibility.

CHAPTER 6

YEP, WE DID THAT TOO!

Note to the reader: Have you ever had "good ideas" that just weren't. Or have you done things quickly, without thinking them through? Or trusted people, and then found out it wasn't the best move? (Yep, these are themes continuing on from the previous few chapters—because they seem to crop up in many of our lives with some regularity.) If so, I think you'll enjoy some of the additional "no, duh" situations we've experienced. I hope you find the following stories to be both helpful and entertaining. Laughing is encouraged. This chapter is SO about the journey.

In the early days of Instagram, we had over one hundred thousand followers on the platform, and after a bit of time, we found that our engagement was low. Even today, I'm no social media maven, and at that time, I had no idea of what low or high engagement should look like. I trusted our team, though, and the consensus was that we needed to "clean up" our list. This meant we would hire a company that would meticulously go through all our Insta-followers and use some type of algorithm (aren't we all a bit tired of that word?) to rid our list of bots, fake accounts, and anything else that was messing with our rhythm, so that our engagement could rise. Sounds like a fantastic plan, right? If you are reading this and shaking your head, keep reading.

I spoke to my children about the cleanup plan, as we often spoke about things within the business that we were doing, especially with something that was as "their generation" as this. They were in their late teens at the time, and they begged me not to do it. There were lots of conversations and passionate pleas, with them insisting that it would be one of the biggest mistakes I would ever make for Dogeared. They just knew that you don't mess with your followers. So much drama! On the other side, I had our Dogeared team assuring me this was the best thing we could do.

The way my family was communicating with me—with all their passion and raging—made it hard to actually hear them. They were young and did not have the experience to speak directly without the raw emotion that drove my decision the other way. What my children said turned out to be so true, and their style of delivery was so tough that all I could see were angry kids, and an angry me. Not people who were frustrated and just wanted to be heard—and who cared for Dogeared as much as I did. Yet another big learning for me.

My decision came down to me and my fear. My fear of not doing what the experts were saying, and them thinking I was not a good leader, over-shadowed my fear of being a C+ mom who doesn't listen to her kids. I had more practice in the not-great-parenting shades of feeling, as outspoken, passionate teenagers will have this effect on the strongest of people.

PEARLS OF WISDOM
Learn to trust your inner voice. The one that
sometimes has to scream to be heard.

During this particular Dogeared chapter, I was not that connected to myself as the leader of our business. I was feeling like so much was outside of my realm of experience, and it was kicking my ass. So much self-doubt led me to not trust the gut feelings that were there. I resigned myself to just needing to ignore them.

We ended up doing the cleanout. And not only did we clean out what supposedly were fake accounts and bots and other scary things that go bump in the night, but we also had our friends, family, and many other people reach out to ask why we deleted them on Instagram.

When I decided to call the "cleaning company" myself and ask them to investigate what happened, they told me that there was no way what I was describing could have happened. When my son—the one I did not listen to—asked me to get some pages of the report so he could evaluate it, he went line by line showing me the real accounts that got deleted. Of course, the "cleaning company" denied it, and my internal team sort of moved on from it, but my family did not. Not for quite a while.

Our family learned a great deal from this incident about communication and resolution through vulnerability, but it was a strain on our relationship for many years as their trust in me trusting them was put in the spotlight. With good reason. This mirrored a dynamic that had taken root in my leadership style at that point: I was trusting in other people and not my own intuition. My intuition had always been my guiding light, and I was off course from the deep trust that I had built the business on.

When the cleaning-up process was done, we had paid for the removal of over 40k followers. And, by the way, if you are a Dogeared fan reading this and remember being blocked for no reason, we apologize. ☺ Please follow us again and we will give you a discount code as our way of saying sorry. @ dogearedjewelry

Ready for another good idea?

———◆———

"Long-term contracts" and "auto-renewing contracts"—these terms immediately make me smile, not smile, and then say, "Hell, no!"

They are money-saving, so they are attractive.

They are presented as the better option.

And they are the way salespeople make good commissions.

So, three words: Don't. Do. It.

When business is flowing along nicely, it's easy to think: *Why not get a five-year contract for everything you might need—from technology tools to office supplies, to medical cabinets with defibrillators on your walls for emergencies, to other necessities. The business NEEDS it, whatever "it" is.*

PEARLS OF WISDOM
It's always a good thing to identify
a need versus a want.
(And yes, you may "need" that
new dress sometimes.)

At a certain point in our evolution, one of our most urgent "needs" was our printers. We worked with a company that leased and managed our many printers, and for a monthly fee, they would service them and bring new toner. At the time, we had about forty-five printers for about 100 people.

When we made the decision to downsize our business and prioritize having fun again, we did not need anywhere close to forty-five printers. We needed just a few. I asked the company we leased from to come and get the majority of the printers, and that is when I learned the specifics of our contract.

Gut punch. We were in a long-term contract that had indeed auto-renewed, meaning of course that because we had not told them *not* to renew the contract, it automatically went into another contract cycle. We had to pay our very large monthly leasing fees as we stared at these printers piled up in the corner . . . sitting idly, not printing.

PURPOSELESS. (Not a word I ever like to use.)

Now, one of the ironic parts is that these were not fancy printers. And as you probably know, printers are *cheap*. We could have bought new ones from an office supply store that we owned and managed ourselves. Nothing like an aging printer in a technologically advanced age to teach you a humbling lesson.

I like to think I am savvier than an auto-renew contract. Obviously, I am not. But taking full responsibility for being in this position meant looking at what I could have done differently and what could be implemented in the future. When it came to departing team members, I could ask the question, "What contracts did you enter into that we will need to manage since you will no longer be here?" And our leadership team could keep a master list of all such agreements they approved. The power of shareable space and documentation can mean not having to go through these kinds of learnings. But we did anyway.

Pearls of wisdom in play big time. Need versus want. As we grow, we sometimes confuse our needs and wants. This is a learning from our long-term business advisor/accountant. There is a big difference between the two. We're excited about not managing everything ourselves. I don't even remember talking to any of our team about the printers, but I can imagine it went something like this: "Who wants to manage printers when there are so many other places to put your attention?" And *boom*, Dogeared was the proud leaser of a bunch of printers.

I finally called the bank that owned the contract and talked to a reasonable human (thank you, universe). I told them (yes, flat-out told them rather than asked) that they could come and get them if they wanted them. If not, I would be donating the printers that I did not yet own. Of course, they did not want old printers that had no value other than the fact that they were leased to us. After many conversations, we made a deal for a final payment to close the contract and be done with the printer chapter. The nonprofit we donated them to was thrilled to have them. They were a big organization that helped people in low-income neighborhoods, so we felt happy to move these printers on to those who could really use them.

The energy flow when the printers left the building was palpable. I think the printers were cheering too.

Part of the reason I believe we were able to close down this contract is that universal timing was in play. We had learned some valuable lessons, and it was time for the next one.

But first, repeat after me:

No auto-renewing contracts! No long-term contracts!
No auto-renewing contracts! No long-term contracts!
Some more fun learnings . . .

———◆———

We were always dreaming up ways for our team to have *fun* and focus on something besides deadlines and work (hello, stress management!). We knew that having fun was a way to welcome their creativity and to connect to Dogeared in ways that sitting at a desk all day would not. This creative quest is how our Green Team was born.

The Green Team was a group of volunteers within Dogeared who were charged with the following: (1) To educate our team on the latest recycling opportunities and regulations, (2) To create a better recycling plan for the company, and (3) To build an onsite community garden. Lots of people wanted to lend a hand. We discovered that we had several gardeners, landscape-design hopefuls, and passionate environmentalists among us. In fact, each time we approached new ideas for Dogeared, we got to see where our team members had skillsets and interests that we might never have discovered without something like this being presented.

We put good resources behind our Green Team dream. Lots of time and lots of money. We built recycling receptacles and placed them throughout our buildings. We made sure people had proper recycling cans for the various types of items they tended to discard. We had company events where we played and designed activities to educate our team about what they could also do more broadly, at work and at home, to help our environment. We gave each person a plant for their desk, t-shirts that said "reduce, reuse, recycle," and had parties at the park with the Green Truck food truck providing us with their yummy vegetarian fare. We were all in!

Our Dogeared community garden was planted right next to our building on city land, and we partnered with a nonprofit school that was in our complex to offer gardening classes and to help us care for it. Within its perimeters, we built garden boxes and created very cool sitting areas. We had edible beauty like local sunflowers and vegetables for salads, which we soon realized were also feeding the local racoons and other wildlife. It was the place to be! There were always people in the garden, which had a ripple effect of good feelings. It was nice, in a soul-nourishing way, to look out the window and see corn stalks swaying in the wind and people enjoying their lunch in this urban oasis.

After about a year of gardening, learning, growing, and generally feeling really good about our environmental stewardship, we had another big surprise. Merlin was at the office late one night at the same time that our cleaning crew was going floor by floor, rounding up the trash and recyclables. He watched proudly as they carefully separated the items, took everything outside to the dumpster area of the complex, and then proceeded to throw it all into the one and only dumpster available.

ONE.

And no green, or brown, or beige labeled cans nestled inside it either.

Just one, plain ole dumpster.

Of course, this led Merlin to further investigate, and it turns out that both our business complex and the city we were in did not have a recycling program.

Um, *what??* Small detail . . . ☺

· · · · · · · · · · · · · · · · · · ·

PEARLS OF WISDOM

Manage the 85% of the business that is in
your control. The other 15% will typically
not be anything you can imagine, so be
gentle with yourself. That 15% may help
you end up with something so much better
than you could have ever considered or
create an opening that is actually needed.

· · · · · · · · · · · · · · · · · · ·

Our fearless Merlin—the leader of the Green Team, environmental conduit for Dogeared and beyond—and his ego were thoroughly *trashed.* (I know, but I had to say it!)

Happily, we found out that we could pay the city for a separate recycling dumpster. So, we did. Dogeared paid for the separate dumpster for our complex (including weekly pickup) until we got the property management to make it right—to share in the costs.

Fast-forward to today and the city mandates it all now, so we have dumpsters of all colors and all creeds. We're now supported at the civic level to help the environment, one piece of trash at a time. We were just a bit ahead of the curve . . . and curves they were.

———•———

OK, another good idea . . . technology. This means in all areas, like account management, sales systems, customer care, websites for both wholesale and retail sales, accounting systems, payroll modules, storage for all of this information, password protection, interface with things like Google, and the many apps that make tech work.

And there needs to be a leader for this technology—someone who understands, who can handle the Tetris puzzle that this produces, and can support the team, the humans, as they work to use everything that technology supports the business with. Technology is also one of the more vulnerable areas of a business, as trust for the team that runs this for your business needs to be pristine. The leader will know everything, because even if there are structures in place for certain teams to only know certain things, there is still someone who needs to know it all and probably even more than it all.

Now, what I have experienced in a very general way about tech professionals is that they are creative, highly intelligent, problem-solving gurus, and yet many of them are not able to communicate well with the people they are supporting. So, when you find someone who can speak tech (understand the technical systems) and can also communicate to the non-technical people in a way we can understand, you have hit gold.

And gold we thought we had found. Our management team hired Richard (not his real name), but out of respect for my husband whose middle name is Richard, we will call him Dick. Dick was a fast-talker who had worked at many impressive places, and his resume sparkled. He seemingly had the coding and fix-it skill sets to keep the Dogeared boat afloat on any given day. He also could talk to people. Our management team liked him and felt his capabilities would get us where we needed to go. (I personally was not sure where that was, but . . .) We tested him out for a week, and I was told he was "the one." Background check, done! References, done! All checked out. We were highly reliant on technology and one small glitch could create chaos. Translation: It was a really important job.

The other thing I learned about hiring these kinds of professionals is that many times they don't like to work regular hours. Some can be night owls, as was the case with our new hire, Dick. So, we said of course, you can work when it's good for you as long as it meets the needs of the business. Our team would send their issues and requests through a portal to Dick and his team to be worked on. Priorities were given to urgent matters so team Dogeared could do what they do. We also had some bigger, long-term initiatives that were being sketched out.

Side note: Before Dick was hired, we were using a highly respected outside company to manage everything for us in our tech world. Their leader talked the talk, and I always felt heard and understood. I believe the team did too. They were creative problem-solvers. This step to hire Dick was part of the management push to take just about everything we did internal, instead of hiring outside companies—supposedly to provide cost savings, more control, and ensure that our bigger initiatives would be easier to manage. Words we loved to hear.

Well, after he passed the three-month trial period (the time we take to assess if we all like each other and see if it's a good fit for the business and the new hire), there were signs that our nighttime worker bees (Dick and team) were having a little too much fun. His company Amex card was exploding with late-night food orders, high-end hotel bills (they had to do all-nighters and needed to nap), and drink deliveries. Yes, "drink" as in cocktails. Party time at Dogeared. Talk about company culture. Ha! So of course, HR and our management team spoke to him about it, and he said that it was just for this particular period of time, as they were working a lot of late nights and finalizing a big project for Ms. Dogeared. OK, I am sure you see the writing on the wall, but I don't think you're anticipating the next thing coming . . .

The expenses kept coming, and the work we were expecting didn't. Things were just not getting done. At all. Dick was formally reprimanded and spoken to a few more times, and we took away his company card. Our team was not being supported, and he was basically lying to us.

If you have ever had to fire someone in the state of California, you know the deal: You need to document like crazy what the employee is doing wrong and build a solid file before you can move ahead with the firing. This is so that if they legally dispute you, you have your facts ready to roll. Insurance companies like this too. I believe it was month five when we were finally ready to say so long to this "party," and that is when Dick decided to show his hand, his masterpiece, what he had been working on all these months. He had taken our systems and Dogeared hostage. He had changed all the passwords and created chaos within our entire technology matrix. He put bugs, and firewalls, and other technological obstacles in play. Remember, he had access to *everything.*

And here it is the big crescendo. He then offered to SELL our own passwords back to us—and for a crazy amount of money. One by one. A total WTF moment. *We were being ransomed!* I know Merlin and I laughed pretty hard. I think we cried too. Who gets to experience something like this? We do!

Fast forward to the finale. We did not end up paying him anything, as (luckily) he wasn't that good at his efforts to sabotage us! That integral tech company I told you about before was able to get into our systems, block him out, and retrieve, through their expertise, most of our passwords. They untangled what he had done. It did take a few weeks. And the fear and stories we made up in our heads about the consequences of being in that position—like Dogeared will be tanked—did give us some sleepless nights. I believe this situation had us using numbers 2, 6 and 7 of the seven principles all at once! Rock a "No Problem" Attitude, Circulate Good, and Trust in Divine Timing and Divine Guidance.

There were a few things that took a little longer, and it wasn't perfect, but no money went to Dick.

And . . . the lessons continue on.

EVEN NOW

After all these years, we still find things that make us scratch our heads. When I recently called Merlin about the following discovery, and we had our laugh, he said, "Oh, that one is for the book!" I agreed, so here it is.

In this time of reinventing the brand, our team is small and mighty, and many of us are wearing many hats. We are lucky to work with a warehouse that ships out all of our product to our customers for both wholesale and purchases from our website. We make our products in Santa Monica, and we then ship them to our warehouse in South Dakota. Having the warehouse located in the middle of the country allows for a shorter lead time to ship to our customers, which means deliveries get there sooner. Plus, the warehouse operators' knowledge and expertise with our systems, along with the requirements of some of our customers, make this a seamless process most of the time. They are good at what they provide for us. That said, sometimes we need to ship directly to our customers from our Santa Monica studio and bypass the warehouse and their expertise. This happens for various reasons—high-value product; something came in late; we're shipping samples; we made a mistake, and the customer did not get the right product the first time; repairs . . . many things. We are usually doing direct shipping two or three times a week.

When we do this, we use shipping portals like the U.S. Postal Service (USPS) and make address labels to put on our shipments. Easy, right? Well, it turns out there is an expertise required here too, which came to light on a beautiful Monday where I got to have a conversation with a very informative woman behind the counter at the post office. But first, a little backstory:

We had a few packages (high-value ones) go missing from our postal shipments. When we looked at the tracking numbers, they read, "Label created, USPS is waiting for the package." Translation: the packages were not showing up in the USPS system even though we (me personally sometimes) had brought them to the post office and put them in the stack of packages on the left side of the counter where all packages wait to go out. This of course ended up costing us money, and, even more importantly, our passion for customer care took a hit. Some customers believed that we hadn't taken their packages to the post office in the first place (which we had), so replacements were sent and more money and resources were spent on shipping them out.

For a time, we changed carriers to United Parcel Service (UPS), as we were not happy with USPS. But then we decided to try USPS again, as it is convenient. I decided that I was going to wait in line and have our packages scanned, so at least they would be in the system, and I also wanted to speak to them about how many missing packages we have had.

OK, now meet Rhonda, our postal expert and lady behind the counter. Rhonda scanned my first box and asked me if there were hazardous materials in the box. When I laughed and said no, she showed me on the box where we had crossed through a line in sharpie that had said hazardous materials.

"Oh, but it's OK, we will fix it for the next time," I responded.

This was her time to laugh.

Rhonda shared with me that because we had accidentally hit a button when making the label that said, "hazardous materials," and because that attached to a bar code on the shipping label, our little sharpie cross-out meant nothing, as that box was being handled like a hazardous material. And here is the part that made me laugh again: hazardous materials are not allowed on airplanes. Kinda makes sense, right? Anything with this designation automatically goes by ground, on a truck, even to somewhere far, far away. A package like this is also considered the lowest of the low, meaning it usually doesn't get scanned at the post office and will only be tracked once delivered. And it could be weeks to months for delivery, as our little jewels survive the hazardous materials handling indignities.

Mystery solved. Our "lost" boxes were probably in transit and might get there in the next month . . . or two.

· · · · · · · · · · · · · · · · · · · ·

PEARLS OF WISDOM

Human error. It's real, it's common, and when
we are looking for answers as to why things
have gone the wrong way, human error
is a good place to lovingly take a look.
Then jump back and hug yourself.
You will make mistakes. You are human.

· · · · · · · · · · · · · · · · · · · ·

You can bet that a memo to all of us at Dogeared who make labels and ship from Santa Monica was circulated. You can bet we laughed a lot too. The smallest details make a big difference. As of right now, we are still waiting to get our "lost" packages delivered. It will be a bonus, as we have already re-shipped and found other ways to make amends to our customers as well.

Now it's a game to see how long a hazardous package takes to get by truck from Santa Monica to Wisconsin. Let the betting begin!

———◆———

Reflecting back on how smart, purpose-driven, doing-good souls sometimes make assumptions, make mistakes, put their trust in the wrong person, or just make decisions that simply don't go as planned, I get to know that thirty-plus years of practice gives us acres of access to all kinds of learning and life. Lucky us? Yes, lucky us.

CHAPTER 7

THE PERFECTLY IMPERFECT PATH TO A MULTI-MILLION DOLLAR BUSINESS

When we began our business, we were using our home in West Los Angeles for all things Dogeared. When it was time to hire our first team member, we wanted to go about finding that person in a way that would be meaningful. Merlin was on the advisory board for the Venice Family Clinic, so we started there. They connected us with Rose (not her real name), a single mom who was working through drug addiction and had just gotten off the streets. Upon meeting Rose, we were head-over-heels. She was passionate about her healing journey, and it felt so natural to welcome her to the family. She was smart and funny, and had a laugh that would get us all going. We were invested from smile one.

That said, the road we set off on together got (very) bumpy soon after bringing her on. We found and furnished numerous apartments for her, and every time, she would need to leave one because someone was bothering her, or because she got kicked out. We were enchanted by her son, who was a toddler at the time, and we helped her find child care for him so she could work. We also paid for his care many times, as managing money didn't make it to the top of her priority list amid total chaos. She was fighting for her life.

If you or someone you love has been caught in the cycle of addiction, you already know what we found out. It is truly one of the most challenging and heartbreaking journeys ever. When Rose was in an especially hard place and didn't show up for work or call, we would panic, and sometimes we were not even sure she was alive. That is a feeling I pray I never experience again. We would use whatever resources we had to help her and get her back on what we considered a healthy path. Even with our support and love, her addiction would win time and time again. She ended up leaving us and coming back a few times, as we just could not say "no." (The art of "no" begins as a learned skill.)

In my happy ending for her, she would have worked for us for thirty years, been sober, happily married or not, enjoyed life to the fullest, and kept us laughing each and every day. It didn't work out that way. The somewhat humorous part is that I thought I had any power to guide her life or her dreams or her journey.

PEARLS OF WISDOM

Preschool is in session—lesson #1:
Even when it seems so much easier
to work on everyone else . . .
I can only work on me.
I can only change me.
I can only heal me.

Rose will always have a piece of our hearts. Our journey with her is one I am grateful for today. She was one of the best teachers ever, as she taught us many unexpected lessons about human suffering, about caring for another with boundaries and self-love intact, and more importantly, about love—the big love that holds it all.

ATTEMPTS AT CRACKING SOMEONE ELSE'S CODE

We spent so much time trying to figure out Rose's life—without the training and tools needed to truly help someone with her challenges—that we felt hurt and sad each time we failed to help her. And we kind of did this on repeat. We would meet people who we were sure we could help by giving them a job, an apartment, money, or the proper expert support like therapy, rehab, etc. We would jump in, sometimes enlist our friends as well (God bless you; you know who you are), and with a "We got this!" attitude, we would take it on!

And sometimes it worked. Yay!

And sometimes it didn't work. Yay?

Our support did not include a precise understanding of the many genetic or non-genetic codes that cause people to stall. We just had a strong sense of wanting to support and really feeling like we could.

What I know without hesitation is that love is foundational to our human condition. We need it to thrive, grow, and live in a purposeful, joyful state. What I have learned from my life's experience is that my love is a small piece of the larger equation.

Self-love is the OG—not only the start to it all, but often the missing molecule when the "sometimes it doesn't work" part comes to pass. Self-love is not something I can wave my magic fairy rainbow wand and create for anyone but myself. Now I have the understanding to say, "No matter how hard I love you, and no matter how much I want it for you, if you don't choose to love yourself and put on your own love-colored glasses, nothing is going to change."

———◆———

A few years ago, our dear Rose came back to visit. Her little toddler was a beautiful man in his twenties, and she was married, sober, and happy. Her genuine wit was back, and we laughed and remembered. Whether or not we knew it at the time, our consistency with her had been something that she counted on, as was the devotion and kindness she experienced with us, as she had not experienced that ever in her life before then. Our time together was important to her and to us. Our love was important to her and to us. Our open hearts were surprising to her, yet not to us.

Love. The superpower.

RAISING JORDAN, RAISING DOGEARED

We hired many people we knew. My sister's boyfriend at the time—a highly talented artist who was in need of some quick cash—would sit in the corner of our living room, cross-legged, headphones in, and bead for hours on end. I had never seen anyone so focused and so fast. One of the best beaders ever. Many others graced our home, and it came to be that only the bedroom I shared with Merlin was Dogeared-free.

Our business was truly a "home business." We took time to connect and to eat lunch together every day, and we were excited to provide lunch to anyone working at the house. We had the coolest vintage stove that I swear made the veggies and rice we made so often taste extra delicious. The pleasure and fun of cooking on it were sauteed into the food. We took the time to enjoy lunch daily, even if for a few minutes. The food was our way of showing some appreciation to the folks who showed up for us.

When we first decided to move Dogeared out of our house and into a studio-type office space, we wanted to be near our home, and near the beach. We most definitely wanted something more interesting than a box in an office park. And we got it.

Welcome to the old mortuary building on Main Street in Santa Monica.

Merlin had his graphics and advertising business in what was the old viewing room upstairs, and Dogeared was in the former embalming space downstairs. There were other businesses there, too, as this location and its history attracted creatives. No crazy energy here. No, not at all. ☺ We "saged" our spaces a lot . . .

PEARLS OF WISDOM

Sage works!
I have always believed in clearing energy in
indoor spaces, as well as the energy in and
around myself and other willing participants,
and I do it on the regular. One way to
positively change energy quickly is to burn
dried pieces of sage or use a smudge stick
of bundled sage. That waft of smoke holds
real power to shift things for the better, a gift
from the ultimate mama, our Mother Earth.

Our team would always gather around
when I did this and ask for a blessing with
sage. It was a fun, not-so-business-like
ritual that we felt honored to share with
each other. Sometimes this would take
me a few hours, when we had multiple
buildings and floors and a team of 150!

Merlin and I felt so lucky that our businesses were in the same building and that we were together as a family. Our son, Jordan, was a baby at that time, and we brought him with us every day. We were obsessed. We could take walks and be with him as he was doing all the cute things that babies do. It was the perfect childcare situation. Cuddling with a baby when you feel stressed or tired puts everything into perspective—restoring calm and flow pretty instantly. For several years, we were blessed to have a woman grace our space and help us raise our family. Merlin and I were an enthusiastic tag team, running up and down stairs all day, as we worked, parented, and checked in with her when Jordan was in her care. We set our lives up well to just enjoy all this newness.

While at the mortuary, we acquired the Dogeared.com domain name. We realized this Dogeared thing, and this internet thing, were both probably going to stick around for a bit. It cost us $7,000, as we bought it from a book trader who owned it. The cool part—and a constant theme in our guided life—was that the amount we paid him gave him enough money to fly home to Scandinavia to see his family. He was so appreciative of the transaction, and we were so grateful he allowed us to purchase it. Synchronicity, yes! Divine guidance and timing had won again!

ONWARD, TO THE RABBIT SHIRE

Dogeared was growing. We had a few more employees, we were selling more and more jewelry, and we were figuring it out as we went. Life felt good—curve balls and all.

Our landlord was sort of an interesting guy and decided that on Christmas Eve he would give us a thirty-day notice to vacate. There was someone else renting space there who was a bit famous and wanted the whole building to himself, so we were out.

So long Main Street . . . and Merry Christmas!

Although Merlin and I would not be working together in the same space again for many years, it turned out, like everything in our life, to be just what we needed. This change allowed us to move our living situation to an incredible property in Topanga, a community in the Santa Monica mountains that people in many creative industries call home. It came complete with a teepee, a creek, and gardens—and all with a mountain backdrop at the top of a *very* windy road. Topanga suited how we wanted to raise our family and gave us the space to enjoy the outdoors and lots of privacy, which has always been something sacred to me.

There was an ideal studio on the property for Merlin to manage his business from. It also allowed our son to have more freedom, as he was mobile now and needed to be on the move. This outdoor playground allowed him all the mud, water, and rocks to throw that a child could wish for. His favorite game was mud monsters, where he and Merlin would be covered in mud and chase each other around the compound. Simplicity at its finest.

The operations of Dogeared moved to Venice Beach. Our address was 483 ¼. I had never had a fraction for an address before. Fractions indicate not whole. Something new to swirl around in my brain. We laughed about it, and our divvied-up new headquarters quickly became dubbed "the rabbit shire." It was a complex of old bungalow-style apartments. I believe there were five buildings that made up the whole complex. We rented a few of the apartments next to each other, and the landlord allowed us to open up (i.e., cut through) the walls to connect the different spaces. The charming result was an internal maze of hallways, doors, and various cubby holes, all randomly strung together.

Where to hold team meetings quickly became a thing. This would require space to think, move, create, and play, which was not space we had in the shire. Our solution was a restaurant down the street with real surfboards as tables whose management allowed us to stay for hours on end. There were always big tips for the servers as we enjoyed our "conference room" and consumed baskets and baskets of French fries. It was a dream.

By this time, Jordan was two years old and had friends in the neighborhood who we did not know. Merlin and I would walk with him, and people would say hello to him by name. He was living his best life. It cracked us up. Turns out, he and his caregiver were famous in the canals of Venice Beach. "Eso parque" ("this park" in Spanish) was what he would say to us when he wanted to go to the sweet local park where he always played. We were steeped in the warmhearted melting pot that defines Venice, and it felt right.

WHAT IT'S ALL ABOUT

As Dogeared grew, we kept adding bungalows, and at one point had taken over two of the buildings completely. With each added team member or next apartment addition, we could physically see and experience the expansion that was happening in our lives on many levels, internally as well as externally. Our "rabbit shire" represented an inflection point, showing us we were running a real business that was right in the midst of momentous growth. Whoa!

One of the buildings we occupied had two floors and included a pulley system that allowed people upstairs to send things to the downstairs without running the rickety stairs all day. This "system" consisted of a bucket and a string. Efficiency, much? Not sure this was "the right tool for the right job"!

We had now moved from holding our team meetings at the restaurant to the outdoor courtyard of the shire. (We got take-out fries, of course!) Sometimes the meetings would spill into the alleyway, with team members dodging cars that drove down the alley. The building wasn't in the best shape, which led to daily conversations about Wi-Fi connectivity, electricity, plumbing, and whether our team would have the basic tools to do their jobs well.

In the absence of certainty, the rabbit shire inspired (read: necessitated) more creative ways of communicating and being with each other. This is where our internal love language was born. We would ask ourselves questions like, "What would Ms. Dogeared do?" She was our integrity marker. We would say, "It's so Dogeared," or "She's/he's so Dogeared!" when encountering the qualities that we associated with someone or something being beautiful, meaningful, connective, and inclusive. Dogeared had become an adjective, noun, adverb, verb, and avatar!

In this circle of good energy, what was becoming clear is that it—Dogeared—was all about connection. It was all about love. It was all about us just being open to whatever would come next. It was all about real presence. This combination of ingredients made up the secret sauce we had discovered that organically found its way into our jewelry and the messages that each piece held. Our customers loved it. And we loved it. Dogeared was about celebrating, mourning, healing, and embracing all of life's experiences.

One of the most popular designs we created was a buddha amulet necklace that was internally named the "get a boyfriend/girlfriend" necklace. There was a sign-up sheet in our studio for those on our team waiting to wear this necklace. It was worn again and again. People wanted to wear the specific necklace that team members before them had worn. The power of that shared energy, strengthening people's abilities to create for themselves, had opened a portal. A portal that created results. It worked! The necklace would circulate through the offices, with its power increasing by getting more and more use. And it would faithfully deliver to its wearer

When we did trade shows, we would take a bowl of sterling-silver word charms and linen string, and we would ask our customers to pick one from the bowl before they started their appointments. These were retailers coming to our booth to place orders. Big chain stores and smaller local stores. We would then tie it on their wrist or neck and have a brief conversation about their "why"—about the meaning underlying the word they chose. Did it make sense to them, or did it feel like a random grab? Did a fun thought accompany their pick, or did they need a hug? The people in our booth could not get enough of this ritual, and it was as good for our team as it was for our customers. (We often had people who were exhibiting their product in other booths hang out in our booth, playing with us like this.) This would often activate tears and laughter and other emotions with our customers, a beautiful and connective energy created before we got down to business. Just like at home and work, inside these convention centers and trade-show halls, connection and love were in the house.

ONE HELL OF A HOBBY

Merlin told me that friends and acquaintances who had not seen us for a while would ask, "Is Marcia still making that jewelry?" It was often asked with an undertone that implied I was in my garage doing my jewelry-making-as-a-hobby (which, to be fair, was an accurate description years before). I think we also could have asked ourselves that question in the same tone as we were just going along, doing our thing, taking the next intended step—all in the flow of the energy we called Ms. Dogeared.

Dogeared was bringing in a few million dollars a year at this point, and it was my full-time focus, so with those cultural markers firmly in place, I guess the answer was, "Yes, Marcia is still making that jewelry."

When we finally moved into a "real" office building, in an office park, I was emotionally worn. I missed our rabbit shire before we even moved out. That funky, seemingly disjointed studio space had been home to so much growth and a richness of experience for us. Those multiple bathrooms, kitchens, and bedrooms—and all that goes with making an old apartment building work on the day-to-day—had provided the spaciousness we needed to get our start in a perfectly imperfect way.

It was soooooooo Dogeared.

Our moves and the places we called home to our business and our lives helped shape what Dogeared is today. Each time we moved, it became evident that it was the external support we needed for what was happening internally. A reflective, holistic approach to business and life that seems to suit us. The combined energy of intention and excitement and joy and love was the connective bridge to creating magic. And magic it was in the sense that it was happening before our eyes, and the mind could not capture the how.

It was happening in the soul space where the mind has no home.

This is how Dogeared got its wings to fly. This is how we, Merlin and I, got our wings to fly. We were entrepreneurs in the flow—not reluctant, or afraid, or shy about what was happening. And Dogeared was *happening*.

When we were doing tens of millions of dollars of business, had over 100 employees, and had purchased two buildings with over 20,000 square feet—this is when the real work began.

CHAPTER 8

C AND ME

Every year, I go with three friends to get our mammograms together. We call ourselves the Square. We make a day of it: lunch, day drinking, mammograms, movies, shopping, and whatever else we can do to play. I love to play. We reframe something that we don't really want to do and make it something that is just part of an already-special day. It was late September 2015, and on this mammogram day, we were just so grateful that we were done, and in our minds, we decided that we were breast cancer-free. Free to enjoy the day!

The next day I got a call from the breast center that had performed the mammogram. "We want you to come in. Something doesn't look right on your scan. We want to do an ultrasound and see if we can get more clarity." It's the call that no one wants. Your stomach flips, you feel like you could throw up, and all you can say is, "Yes, what time?" Breast cancer runs in my family. My mom has had it, my mom's mom died from it—it's a thing with my ancestry. It's a big thing.

Merlin and I went in the next day. They did the ultrasound and found *something.* "It's something that should not be there. We need to do a biopsy," they said. "You can schedule once insurance approves it. Maybe you can get in next week." After that all I heard was *blah, blah, blah, blah, blah.*

Waiting. This was something that I was not used to and a lesson I would encounter a lot on this journey. God bless my beautiful husband for loving me as he does and having a knowing that the waiting alone would damage all parts of me/ us. He went and did his Merlin thing, in the nicest, most firm way, with no options besides what he was asking: *to do the biopsy right then.* Then as now, he is my protector, my man. His strength translates to my strength.

Success. Things fell into place.

We went to lunch while waiting for the biopsy. I remember that I was cold. Merlin was holding my hand, hugging me, rubbing my feet, and just doing anything to calm my anxious system. After a few hours, they did the biopsy. It stung a bit, and we were done. The results would come soon.

———◆———

I showered for a long time that night, working to get the stain of the day off me. My inner sense knew I had breast cancer, even if the world had not said it out loud yet.

For the next few days of waiting for the results, the energy around me felt opaque and heavy. Being busy was what I did, so I focused on Dogeared—my playground. Anything to distract. When my doctor called, Merlin and I held hands as he said the words.

"You have breast cancer. Stage 2a, lobular breast cancer."

I hung up, looked at Merlin, and knew I needed to get out of there. Like now. This was the only time I remember not wanting to be in my Dogeared studio.

One of the things I dreaded the most was having to tell people. It's just a weird space to be in. You want the people in your life to know, but at the same time, it's painful holding their pain as they hold your pain. It's just a circle of no one knowing what to say—and all that pain; it is not the kind of circle that I typically like.

My son was away at school, so we called him to let him know. Being far away from him, I wished I did not have to say those words into the phone. We cried. He asked if he should come home. We went by my daughter's school on our way home to let her know. She walked towards us flanked by her friends, and she knew. We held each other and cried, and I let her know I was going to be OK, which in my soul I knew without a doubt. We called other family members on the way home, and it hurt. There was so much fear and sadness with everyone.

I was just doing what I knew needed to be done. It sucks to tell people you love and who love you that you have cancer. The word *cancer* is terrifying. You can have cancer and be told you are going to die. You can have cancer and be told you will be OK. And there's so much space in between for fear to creep in. Fear of the unknown. Fear of pain. Fear of losing your freedom. And the list goes on. I was in the "going to be OK category," which of course is the team you want to be picked for.

———◆———

When we got home that night, the Square and the husbands came over. We hugged, we cried, we laughed, we drank wine, we ate takeout, and we sewed my love pillow. Love pillows are the brilliant work of one of my closest friends. They're beautiful pillows with the word "love" on them that go to people who may need a little extra love. Once you get your powerful love boost from the pillow you've been given, you pass it onto the next worthy person. I would be the recipient of one powerful pillow that shadowed me on my entire breast cancer journey. One of my dear friends has mine right now as she too takes on the breast cancer journey. She told me that we may be in a custody battle over the pillow once she is healed, and I assured her it was all hers!

Being in this environment was distracting in all the best ways. Our house was filled with the energy and love that makes our house our home—something stable and something I can count on. Something familiar. This was especially important as I knew that everything would be changing. I stayed as present that night as I could to savor the normalcy of the evening, even though what brought us together was something that made us all sad. Really sad.

Fear was not present that night. Uncertainty was there, but Love was the queen that night, with her beautiful people, food, wine, and pillows—all together, a big blanket of love that does not allow fear under her covers.

———◆———

Before my diagnosis, I was proud of my superwoman powers. I ran my company and raised my kids with love and everything I had in me. I was married to a beautiful man with whom I shared a great love affair. I played hard and big and had strong friendships. I did good in the community. I needed very little sleep and was one of the most productive people I knew. I loved how I showed up in the world. On paper, good stuff, right? And yet my body had allowed this to happen, calling me to explore what needed some attention, from a psychological perspective. Deep dives into all things me. Cancer is one of those things that invites you to look at it from all angles, and if you choose to do the looking it's like an E-ticket ride at Disneyland—admission to one of the bigger rides in the park, like the Matterhorn, or any of the rides that are up and down and all around, the ones where you are screaming out loud as you simultaneously surrender to what is so.

The rollercoaster was off and running. Soon there were appointments with many doctors, opinions, and more opinions. A few weeks of learning and listening while I was gathering my medical team. Meanwhile, cancer was still in my body, which I did not like. I was ready to have that thing out the minute they told me it was in there, but you can't just do that. Getting the plan together requires the backup of many tests and lots of data-gathering: your ancestry, age, weight, type of cancer, how active you are, and many other factors. And then there's the act of comparing you to the studies that have been done to see where you fit and what will give you the best healthy result. Of course, my cancer recovery was not a slam dunk. I was in the gray zone, so I relied heavily on the expertise of my team to make good decisions about my care, so that I could then make good decisions about my care. What I decided early on was this was my journey, and I was in control of certain things, including who I made decisions with about my path. I was beyond lucky as I had excellent health care. Team Marcia, thank you!

Strapped in for the ride, my time was no longer free. I felt trapped, so I played the game I knew to play. I understand that freedom is a mindset and decided to lean into the essentials. I stayed present. I smiled a lot. I hugged. I got used to the routine of heading to appointments and being grateful if it didn't hurt that much, or if the technician was kind, or people smiled at me, or if I got quick results. Small victories like this were everything.

I was told that I was lucky the mammogram picked it up, or rather, that the head of radiology who read my chart that day picked it up. Lobular cancer is hard to detect. You can't typically feel it. And because it's slow growing, many times, by the time it's detected, it's not a good scenario.

The day I got my lumpectomy, my family and my Square were waiting for me when I got out. They had crystal bindis (decorative dots) for our foreheads—small adornments reminding us of the bigness of our inner light. People in the waiting room were smiling at us. The beautiful energy of us loving each other was contagious. When I went into the pre-op room, I was shivering. I was scared. The last thing I remembered is my surgeon holding my hand until I drifted off. I have since shared with him and his nurse what a beautiful moment in my experience with humanity that was. He helped me cross a threshold into healing while holding my hand. The power of a kind gesture, being a good human being, and understanding the impact of holding my hand, of true connection.

I have since held many a stranger's hand—mostly on airplanes with women who are scared of flying. There are lots of us. When my kids were young, I used to not love flying either, so I understand how that fear can manifest. Most recently I got to experience the hand-holding magic on a nine-seater propeller plane from Nantucket to Boston. The woman behind me was crying, terrified of this tiny little plane. There was lots of hand-holding in this mid-air moment, with a few other women and I talking with her and soothing her—and big hugs at the end. We had created a community within the span of forty-five minutes. Yes, it can happen. Compassion, connection, and helping each other. A spiritual trifecta!

And then the tumor was out. I was cancer-free. Even for a minute, I was cancer-free—to me, the most important words in existence! Now I was going to be on a journey that would require me and my positive attitude to make it happen. I needed to do the work both physically and spiritually to heal, and to never again let my DNA think that it needed to let cancer in.

After many hours of conversations, including discussion about percentages and a particular chemo being quite tolerable, the recommendation was made. It would be chemo for a few months, radiation every day for seven weeks, and then an anti-estrogen pill regime, as my cancer was estrogen-positive. I was in for the Western medicine route, along with a few Eastern medicine sprinkles and some real shifts in my spiritual psychology.

Everyone wants to hear they just need radiation. Chemo is a bigger and scarier concept—part of the list of C words that no one wants to hear. No one wants to be sick, lose their hair, and burn out their insides while eradicating microscopic cells that may or may not be there, and the list of "don't-want-to's" goes on. I did have a choice as to whether to do the chemo or not. I chose to give myself the best chance of being one and done, so chemo it was.

On the morning of my first day of treatment, I walked down to the beach and put my feet in the cold water. The anti-inflammatory, healing water. I went down in prayer, asking for a smooth ride, asking for it to not make me sick, asking for my next chapter to play nice. Before all this, I was someone who did not even like taking Advil. I was proud to check the box on any medical paperwork that I was not on any medication. Times had changed. My mind needed to wrap itself around and generously receive all the care I would be given—with my acceptance and ultimate surrender to *what is* at play. Trusting in the bigger power and picture. Trusting in my family and friends and trusting in myself.

I arrived with my gang. The Square, my daughter Grace, and Merlin. I held my palms out and thanked the chemo for doing what it was going to do and allowing me more time in this body and soul. When the first IV line went in, I cried. They were tears of relief that I was lucky enough to have health care, and love, and that I was on the side of healing now. Chemo created that bridge for me. This particular C word was on my side, in a very odd pairing. I cried every time they started the chemo, all with the same feeling of gratitude and a little bit of fear. Receiving has never been easy for me. I even have trouble twisting both of my hands up into the receiving position. My cancer journey to this point had already changed so many things within me. This was full, on-my-knees surrender.

In my treatment area we played games and caught up on headlines in magazines we never read. We bought stock, we started an Instagram for our dog, and we bought some artwork online. We laughed, and they kept me focused on accepting rather than being afraid. All emotional jitters were smoothed by the sweetness and love of these humans who cared for me.

We brought gifts of Dogeared jewelry, homemade bread, love pillows, and other treats to share with whoever was there that day. We left the doctor who read my initial mammogram a basket of Dogeared with a thank-you note. His expertise saved my life. He called us and said no one had ever thanked him before. I would have the opportunity to live because of his eye—*thank you!*

Throughout the many weeks of treatment, my friends and family continued to go in the chemo ward, so we would gift the nurses and other patients. I was attached to the dripping IV bags and could not walk around, so my friends would come back and report on who they met, what their story was, and what jewelry or gift each patient picked. Dogeared has always been about messages of hope, love, and connection. In the beginning of my cancer journey, giving in this way was the lifeline that gradually opened a door within me to receiving. But it was about more than me as well. It felt like everyone involved was in the full flow of this life force—the flow of giving and receiving that takes place universally for all people if we believe and trust in it.

At this point, I also decided to see about saving some of my hair. We found a system called a cold cap that works to freeze your hair follicles as the chemo is sending its signals through your system. We were lucky enough to get Michael as our cold-cap guy. His wife had been through cancer a few times, and he was a wonderful addition to our treatment room. We dubbed him Archangel Michael, as his task was big—I had a lot of hair, and the process required great precision and timing. There were days when I would touch my hair and clumps would fall out, but throughout all the chemo, the protocol worked for the hair on my head. I had enough hair left that if you didn't know me you would not really notice those areas where the clumps came out. I lost most of the other hair on my body. My lack of eyebrows shocked me every time I looked in the mirror. Every time. Also, because the cold cap doesn't allow you to dye your hair, I got to see what my gray would be like if I grew it out. This picture was not what I had envisioned. I always dreamed of the long, white-gray hair of the goddess ladies when the time would be right. Not so much.

After each chemo session I would have two OK days, and then I would feel it coming. I usually had enough warning that I would take some of the medicines they gave me and hibernate—allowing me to sleep for twelve hours straight. Blackout sleep. I came to know the drug combo that would give me this sleep. When I would wake up and be burning up from the chemo doing its job, I would sit outside in my backyard in the winter California months, wearing a T-shirt and underwear. Merlin and Grace would wrap up in big blankets and lie outside with me. Meditation music on and nowhere to be except right where I was. When it was nighttime, I played with the moon, and she with me. Present, like never before. I also had my oncologist's cell phone number, and he made it clear to call anytime with any question—saying that if he did not call back within five minutes, to call him back. *Earth Angel.*

I was lucky in my chemo experience. The doctors had done their work, and so had my body, so it was relatively straightforward in medical terms. Four treatments. Check. My body was tired. She had worked hard, and as with when I gave birth, I had a beautiful appreciation for her abilities, her stamina, and for what an incredible cosmic machine she was. As my yellow-green pallor slowly faded, my rosacea was a welcome friend, bursting back on the scene, brightening up my face.

During chemo, I actually did have people say that I looked "greenish" while in conversation with me. Like I had a choice. Oh yeah, I did have a choice, and that greenish tint was hard earned, like a badge of honor. I had done it. I chose to improve my chances of non-recurrence by a few percentage points by enduring, embracing, and finishing chemo. I was beyond lucky to have health insurance and people who cared for me. I send love to anyone who must manage this, especially those without the means or health care. I used to cry a lot thinking about this—about anyone who would have to endure cancer without being able to make a choice about their healing journey because they did not have insurance or people to care for them. During my treatment, Merlin and I chose to support someone going through cancer by providing them with a cold cap, which at the time was expensive and not supported by health insurance. Archangel Michael arranged this for us. We gave someone *choice.* We gave someone the opportunity to have hair. You would think there would be mental health support for anyone going through cancer. That to me would include the right to keeping your hair. Dogeared has always raised money for different organizations through the sale of certain products, and breast cancer became something that I now had the experience to understand in a new way. I was grateful to have an outlet to create awareness. Dogeared just doing her thing one more time!

Next up was radiation—every weekday for seven weeks. I got my first tattoo as they marked the spot where they would direct the machines. I always thought my first tat would be some kind of rock 'n' roll wings, but a dot it was. I felt lucky that I got to lie facing up and not confined by a mask, a tube, or anything that strapped me down. The radiation room had lots of paraphernalia that did not come my way. I was beyond grateful for that. It was just me and the whirring of machines that would help to ensure that no bad cells went anywhere in my body, that my body was clean of cancer.

I did acupuncture throughout most of my treatments to calm the side effects. Generational wisdom from a family of healers that I know provided me with the support that made all this tolerable, and sometimes even joyful. Tiny needles precisely placed to help my body heal, my hormones settle, and my side effects lessen, especially the nausea and exhaustion. Incredible laughter and kindness and support from this team. The primary doctor's family has been healing people for generations. This is part of his DNA. He gave me the ability to see and feel joy in the simplest terms—eating, walking the beach, laughing, or being awake for a good part of a day. The hardest part of the radiation was going there every day for a five-minute treatment. And someone was with me every time I went. So many hours throughout this healing journey dedicated to me. This nurturing was almost as hard to receive as the time that the treatments took. Surrender and receiving, two things I was getting better and better at. I felt loved. I also felt exhausted and a little burnt where the radiation was focused. Upon my radiation graduation, there were gymnastics in the waiting room, and a certificate. One that's not hanging on my wall quite yet.

Then came the final step: taking a little pill to manage my estrogen. What a job that is. No estrogen = no food for the cancer = a life without cancer. *Easy enough.* About four years into taking it, I was experiencing some things physically that were new, and I wanted to find out if they were common. Shortness of breath, heart palpitations, *and* I was not able to dance up hills, which was the thing that really made me want to do something about these symptoms. Anyone who knows me knows that going uphill is not my favorite thing, but hiking is, so my reframe is that I dance. I dance up hills. Loud music in my air pods and the dancing hits my soul. "Dances with hills" could be my secret spy name. Mess with my dancing and I am going to figure it out. This is when my investigation of the side effects was launched, and I must say, this is really where Google is not your friend. I only went online one time to do my research and allowed myself twenty minutes. My heart broke wide open for what women go through to live cancer-free, pain-free lives. I was devastated. Women who have already endured so much and then go on to deal with debilitating joint pain, loss of hair and extreme moods, which lead to relationship issues, and so many other hurts. Add the mental strain of managing all of this while working to be cancer-free. This is where I throw my hands up in the air and say, "Really?"

In my case, the side effects lessened on their own. At the time of writing this book, I have a few more months to hit my five-year mark of taking the little pill, which is when it ends. Hormones are so important, and I am excited to see what my body does this time when she gets to make estrogen again.

———◆———

Six months of my life dedicated to my life. My daughter speaks about one of her favorite times with me during this process. We were sitting together and laughing, watching a television show. It wasn't the show that she loved, but rather the uninterrupted time with me. Just being present, holding hands. In my canopy bed that had been draped in notes from people who loved me. I kept those notes up for months after my treatments were done. A bed drenched in love. Sometimes one of the notes would fall off the string to the floor, and I would know the angels were wanting to share a message with me.

I have always felt connected to my angels. When I was newly pregnant with my son but had no idea, I walked by a rack of cards and a "congratulations on your new baby" card flew at my feet. My life is full of connections like this. Some are gentle and some are not. I prayed on a full moon for health, and then a month later was diagnosed with breast cancer, ultimately giving me the health I had asked for. We all have this ability to see; we just need to be open to seeing.

When I first found out about my cancer, I started working with a person who I thought was going to be a real teacher, one who would take me to a faraway land and have healers work with me to make it all better. I wanted a quick fix. My perspective now is that I took some interesting and fun trips, connected to some amazing women, and really found the power within myself to create a life that was good even in the depths of a cancer journey. What I learned most during this time was that no one has the power to change or guide my life except me. (This is THE big pearl of wisdom!) This is all me. Self-love, self-care, self-trust, and self-empowerment. These are the "S's" I now choose to guide all things me.

The radiation, chemo, and subsequent pill therapy were all insurance policies for me. They gave me a bit more advantage, and I'm in gratitude for the chance to live cancer-free. I realize it's not a choice everyone has. Freedom and choice. I was the luckiest girl on the planet, *and* my hair was growing back. (As I'm writing this book, I have decided to grow my hair down to my butt. My daughter is asking me why? Because I can. Freedom and choice!)

I can say with all my heart that I gave a lot to this journey. It was the start to many things mystical and magical, stemming from me and my soul, and my willingness to grow and learn. My biggest learning was that I was powerful beyond all imagining.

CHAPTER 9

love, mmc

During my breast cancer journey, I decided to write email letters to my friends, family, and team to give them updates as to where I was physically, how I was doing, next steps, and anything that I felt needed some conversation. It was a streamlined way for everyone to know what I knew.

It also allowed me some spaciousness around my healing. I believe it was a powerful way to check in with myself and where I was with the many balls that were in the air.

When it came time to revisit these letters in the process of writing this book, I did not do it with anything but a sense of power. There was no critiquing and judging myself. I worked hard to lead with love during this time, hard being the "key" word. I worked to not let fear guide anything. It wasn't a perfect process. I was in practice. This was the Harvard of practice.

"love, mmc" is my quick sign off and on. Marcia Maizel-Clarke. I typically write all my correspondence like this—with no capital letters and very little punctuation. I just go. It's one of my signature Marcia things. I'm not sure when it started, but it's easy and allows me to flow.

I wrote this stream of correspondence from a place of presence and a knowing that I would be OK. Not everyone is so lucky. If my letters and their themes can help anyone in any way navigate this uncertain place, then those chosen for this book have earned their spot. It was a conscious decision not to put much more into this chapter than the letters themselves, as I believe that they alone are enough.

Subject: me!

hi!

just got home from the doctor. i am
healing really well.

i am cancer free!! they got it. all
my margins were good—woohoo! it was
3.5 cm, not 1.3. i am stage 1c. this
kind of cancer has a bunch of little
tentacles that kind of join together,
thus the 3.5. doctor is super happy
that the margins were all clear!

they took 3 nodes. 1 had cancer, 1 had
200 cells of cancer (which in cancer
land is teeny) and 1 was clear. this
puts a little spin on my treatment plan
because of that second node—nothing

dramatic, just choices to make once i
meet with an oncologist. they ordered
a test that works with the tissue they
already took, and this helps tell if
the cancer will come back etc.… amazing
new test!! will help me make decisions—
if it was one node, no chemo would be a
big option. because of the cancer one,
still could be the same as one, but we
will see what the experts say.

what this means is that i will have
options for my prevention plan! i am
still thinking radiation (they can
radiate my arm pit too—no need for
laser hair removal now!) and maybe an
anti-estrogen pill. that's what i am
pushing for!

i meet with 1 oncologist tomorrow and
another in a few weeks.

i am super super happy!!! again,
feeling supported by the world around,
and just being in the flow of this whole
thing. cancer free!!!!!! nothing better
to my ears…

love to you all!
xxxxmmc

Subject: where i am at!

hey there!

just wanted to give you an update on my
journey—

i am in a healing/waiting phase right
now. i am healing well. i do get tired
a bit more easily, but i am 2 weeks out
of my surgery, so i think this is to
be expected. i have been walking a lot,
and working out as usual, so that feels
good! mentally i am peaceful, open and
in a very spiritual place.

my goal with all of this is to make
a decision based in science and
spirituality, since the latter is much
more comfortable to me.

i have two appointments next week that
will help determine the course of
my prevention plan. i am also still
waiting on 2 different sets of tests
that will help me make the decisions
ahead. thinking they should be in next
week. the science coming in hot!

i got good news this week, that they
don't want to remove all my lymph nodes

with more surgery, as they feel other
things will accomplish the same result.
yay!!!!

the spirituality—

-it's interesting that when the blood
moon was here a few months back (the
supercharged full moon), i held hands
with my girls and sourced health. the
blood moon was all about shaking things
up, it was a disrupter. i think it's
interesting that a health shake-up is
just what i got, big time!!!

the past full moon a few days ago was
all about grounding ourselves and
aligning ourselves with what we truly
love. it's about letting go of what is
not working and embracing the truth
in our hearts and healing all that is
here. i am so excited about this one!!!

i will keep you posted as to what
happens next but did not want you to
think that my silence was anything but
good, peaceful healing time!!!

xxxmmc

Subject: me!!

hi!
so, after much consideration, i have
decided to do chemo, radiation, and the
anti-hormone therapy. lots went into
the decision and i know it's the right
one for me. it's all about prevention!!
my chances for non-reoccurrence were
very high with just the radiation and
anti-hormone, but the chemo pushed me
into the 90th percentile of no re-
occurrence, so i took those 5% points
that chemo offered. it was all about
the lymph nodes…since a few of them
had cancer in them, and even a little
bit outside of them (surgery got all
of this!), chemo was needed to make
sure no other little molecules escaped
anywhere in my system.

it will be 4 rounds of chemo, one
every 21 days, wait 3 weeks and then
start probably 4-5 weeks of radiation.
after that the anti-hormone therapy
will begin. i have been told that this
chemo is very well tolerated, and i
know i will be well supported and
in a meditative zone for the coming
months. i also will be doing lots of

acupuncture and herbs as you know i
love this and it helps with it all a
great deal. you know i will be working
with my healers too—i am so lucky to be
surrounded by such powerful souls.

they have a cool new ice cap that keeps
your hair—it basically puts your hair
follicles to sleep—pretty genius. for
sure going to give this a go!

i am not sure when i am starting yet,
probably in the next few weeks. i need
to have a few more tests done and then
the fun will begin.

i am in a good place with all of this.
i am happy, grounded, and looking
forward to all the learning that will
come. spiritually i am in the best
place i have been in a long, long time.

once i know more, i will let you know—

i have a favor to ask all of you—when
you think of me, picture me in 10
years, skinny dipping on the beach and
sipping some far niente wine, with all
of you running in with me!! i need the
good positive love.

no worrying!! the worrying puts worrying
ju ju on me, and right now it's better
to imagine me laughing, imagine me with
long beautiful hair—dancing with all of
you!

i love you all very very much.

xxxxmmc

Subject: me!

hi there!

second chemo, check!

i am doing well. we had another chemo
yesterday. started my day going to the
beach and putting my feet in the water
and sand. sent some of my hair out into
the ocean and watched the gorgeous
sunrise. open-eye meditation—i opened
my heart and my hands to release and to
receive. miracle one.

lost a lot of hair right before my
treatment—it's normal, but i luckily
still have a ton of hair! that big
frizzy, curly hair that for most of
its life has been tamed, keratined,
colored, cut, blow dried, aqua netted,

flat ironed and more, is now my best
friend. i talk to it and give it love
every day, and since with the cold
cap treatment you can't do any of the
above, it's in its most natural state,
and i love it. miracle . . .

i feel good this morning. did not
sleep very much last night, but i know
lots of sleeping is ahead, as i get
my Neulasta shot today. dr. is going
to lower my dose so i may not ache as
long. the ache is manageable, just like
a bad flu, so i am not worried at all.
ready to watch movies, and sleep, and
be in my lovely bed, and grow!! i get
to grow lots of new cells, and my body
is strong and is doing this so well. i
love my body, she is doing her thing
with grace and beauty. another miracle.

archangel michael was there to cold cap
me again. he was not supposed to be
with us, but rearranged his schedule so
he could come hang with us again—love
his precise nature, and military timing
on making sure my hair has its best
chance to succeed! (he has to change
the -40 degree cap 12x!) plus he is a
good crossworder, miracle michael . . .

yesterday—my gang was all there—maggie,
laurie, jacqui, grace, and merlin (my
rock). once they did the blood tests
and deemed my blood healthy and good,
we got the party started. i again
cried when they put the chemo in, as
it's such a release of gratitude for
me . . . i am so grateful to be going
through this with all the love and care
i am getting. miracle miracle miracle

miracles of the day—

merlin gave some of my hair to the
little birdies in the back yard for
their nests—i think they will like the
length and color! love that he thought
of this.

we got to see some of the same
beautiful ladies that were there last
time, such strength.

my jewelry fairies gave out jewels to
everyone there. dogeared always makes
people happy—which in turn makes me happy.

we bought stock—the new cold cap
company that made the computerized one
was fda approved the day before, so we
all jumped on it.

we got creative and made a new insta
for dogeared and frankie (our cutest
dog) grace was the expert here, helping
us be current and cool!

caught up on all the trash mags—we now
know who is the sexiest man alive, and
who is not.

had an amazing lunch—soup and bread
seem to be my thing there.

i got a mani from maggs—dark nails are
good to have during this particular
chemo, she is an excellent manicurist.

my altar was there with my lotions,
potions, oils, flowers and i was
pampered—

we watched videos of people getting
pets for presents—highly recommend.
jacqui is an expert at finding these
types of things.

we listened to some inspiring music.

we did a crossword—haven't done one is
years, i think there is a reason.

i got pot pills!!! dr. really working
on the stomach stuff, as that was my
biggest issue last time. new regime for
any stomach issues includes some pot
pills. more fun!

i love you,
mmc

**Subject: love + celebration + great
bread**

fourth and final chemo—wooooooohoooooo!

hope you all have a few moments as this
one is the finale, and there is lots to
share . . .

yes, i am up early, but i fell asleep
around 8:30 last night, as the night
before i had only slept for an hour.
steroids, a good book i could not put
down, excitement for #4, and a need for a
bowl of cereal in the middle of the night
all contributed to the no sleep night.

started my day with a phone call from
jordan giving me love as he is back at
school. so connected to me with this
journey. love him!

then of course, at the beach. sitting on
the sand berm, as the tides are so high
right now. meditations of releasing and
receiving, feet in the sand, laughing,
and i climbed down the berm to get my
feet into the water for that release too.
cold, anti-inflammatory feet taking me to
number 4!!!

about yesterday—i feel it should be
coined the "love festival." my love
squad was there—grace, merlin, maggie,
laurie, and jacqui, and archangel
michael (cold capper) and they made
this a finale to never forget.

about a week ago, we started talking
about what to bring to give out to the
nurses and patients that we get to see
every three weeks. we had given lots of
jewels, and totes—so it was decided we
should do love pillows. this is a crazy
idea because of timing, as love pillows
require a great deal of stitching,
sewing, cutting, and creativity.

a little history on the love pillow—

3 years before, i had a hysterectomy
(huge fibroid that grew too big because
of my being in the fast lane, not

wanting to stop and listen, and having
too much "fear" about surgery etc.).
maggie made me a "love pillow" to bring
with me to the hospital and on the
journey. it's hand sewn, has the words
"love" stitched on one side, down-
filled pillow that is cuddly, soothing,
and just the perfect gift. i felt it
protected me, gave me something to hold
on to all the time, and i put the love
side toward my body and knew my body
was being extra loved. i kept that
pillow basically glued to my person
while i was healing.

afterwards we felt that the love pillow
should keep healing, so we sent it to a
friend who was in a healing place. then
it came back, then we sent it out again
to another friend, and so on and so on
and so on. each time the pillow picked
up the beautiful healing energy from
the beautiful person who had it before
so that pillow is now one powerful
energy source.

many more have been made and sent too.
on the night of my initial diagnosis,
my crew and their hubbies came over,
and we basically drank (a lot), ate,
and made a new pillow for me (as my

original was traveling), and a few more
that were needed to be sent.

So . . . love pillows it was. many
chipped in a little with the sewing
(meaning sewed one pillow's letters),
and laurie and maggie did the heavy
lifting and basically hand sewed 15
pillows to share with the people
in chemo yesterday. maggie being an
amazing interior designer and fabric
saver extraordinaire had the most
incredible fabrics to create these
from.

i am pretty much stationary when i am
getting my treatment and cold capping,
so the girls would go out, give a few
pillows, and come back and tell me the
story of the giving. let's just say
yesterday was also a cry festival too.
i basically cried after each story, as
the receiving was so moving.

one of my favorites is the older
man whose arms were so bruised and
battered, who asked them how much they
cost, and when he was told he could
just pick one, he plopped that thing
right under both his arms and was so
happy. immediate healing! so many

stories and people were blown away. the
nursing team kept coming in to tell
us how much joy was being created. my
squad created pure joy in a room that
sometimes doesn't feel joyful. it was
magic!!!

good bread—so jacqui's husband has his
own sourdough starter for bread that
he created many years ago. his bread
is like eating what you would imagine
eating a slice of heaven is. it is
divine. jacqui brought bread, salt,
and butter for us to eat, as well as
beautiful baggies of the same for
the patient's getting treatment, with
instructions on how to heat it up later
if they did not eat the whole thing
right there! so, after people got a
pillow, my squad went back out to give
out the bread! seriously insane!!! my
doctor, who has sworn off bread, could
not even resist! he had a huge smile on
his face—bread makes people smile.

smart eyes—last week maggie took me to
an ophthalmologist as i thought i was
having teary eyes all the time and my
oncologist wanted me to get it checked
as one of my chemo's— Taxotere (isn't
it funny that the word tear is in this

word)—can have long-term side effects
of this type of thing. turns out i have
dry eyes and lovely mucus which makes
it feel like i have wet eyes. no long-
term issues, and the recommend is warm
compresses and over-the-counter tears,
which she said i should be using during
chemo as it helps the side effects
from becoming anything but short-term.
maggie pointed out that the miracle of
my body is that she knows that i needed
my own tears during chemo, as every
time they give me my first chemo bag i
cry. how brilliant is my body!! she was
well teared yesterday—

i was giddy going into this treatment
as it was the last stop on what is
supposed to be the harder part of my
healing. so giddy in fact that my poor
nurse could not find a vein to hook
into, i was too amped. maggie had to
come in hold my hand, and i had to do
some deep breathing and warm towels and
the third poke was the charm.

once the first chemo was rolling, and i
was crying, my squad gathered around
me, held hands and they sang and hummed
what they know of celebrate me home, by
kenny loggins. (old history with kenny,

with me kissing him on stage during
college on an hbo special . . . ha!) so
his music is near and dear to me. we
were all so present and so connected.
when about an hour later they played
the same song on the phone, i cried
again and we held hands. so beautiful.

wonderful lunch and gracie (maggie's
daughter and my grace's bff) delivered
it to us. so grateful she is home from
college and was able to visit!

jacqui kept us laughing our asses off
yesterday. i could do many paragraphs
on this alone—jacqui just found out
she is going to be a grandma. like 2
days ago found out. her daughter is
pregnant. hasn't even seen a doctor
yet pregnant, and jacqui (her grandma
name will be nona) has already bought
clothes for her granddaughter (yes, she
just knows it is a girl), had paintings
commissioned, videos she has saved
for years that she is now sending,
picked out houses to buy for them in
ohio, picked out name, you get the
picture. our jacqui is one of the most
passionate, jump-in-with-all-of-her-
clothes on women we know.

we looked at magazines, booked hotel
rooms for a friend's daughter's wedding,
ate a lot of snacks, had a whole laugh
and cry over ugly crying, and tried to
"pretty" cry (not possible), booked my
hair appointment for three months from
the day, as that is when i can have my
first color and blow dry!!! (my hair is
rockin' and doing her thing!) we had
offers from other patients of rooms
in santa monica in their homes if for
some reason i can't get to my radiation
appts (because the highway goes out),
future dinner invites, and lots of hugs
and kisses all around.

i have been eating like crazy the
last week or so. my body knows she is
going into hibernation mode and is
stockpiling! the next week to 10 days i
will mostly sleep and not eat. this is
how my body truly heals itself. i also
am ready with all my western meds to
manage any/all side effects.

one of the last things at treatment we
did was pull my angel cards. maggie
handed me the deck, and she decided to
just open the angel card book at the
same time that i pulled a card. i only
pulled one card (usually i pull 4).

she opened the book to "soulmate," and
the card I pulled was soulmate! angels
having fun with us.

hmmm . . . another cry. my soulmates
were all around me. i was floating . . .

my last cry of the day was from a card
that grace left on my bed—she sees me,
and what a gift this journey has been
for us as mother and daughter.

today i head to get my Neulasta shot—
the one that helps my cells come back
and gives me the growing pains. lots of
growth here.

i also today get mapped for my next
part of my healing journey of radiation
for 7 weeks. everyday quickie appt. i
start the radiation in about 3 weeks.
this is pinpointed to just my surgical
areas and gets any cells that may have
escaped during surgery. it's again a
precaution i am choosing to do.

thank you for all of the love, gifts,
cards, encouragement and pureness you have
all given so freely. so much love in one
life, i am crying again. go eyes go!!!

love you all madly.

xxxxxmmc

Subject: the journey!

hey everyone!

thought it was time for an update from
healing central—

i am in my third week of radiation. i
go every day to santa monica and see
earl, who is responsible for moving me
into perfect position, along with joey
who manages what earl does and actually
pushes the button for the machines to
do their thing. i love when joey gets
me into the "perfect" position, and she
says "perfect" about 2-3 times. it's
something you like to hear when you
are laying with your arms above your
head and getting ready to receive your
radioactive superpowers. i have a
total of 7 weeks, so i should be able
to fly with my superpowers at the end
of this. it's an easy process at this
point in the healing!

tho appointment is only about 15
minutes long, with about 3-5 minutes of

the machines doing their thing. i close
my eyes and seem to go into a meditative
place, or even a little nap. earl always
is the one to come in and let me know i
am done, and half the time i don't even
hear him come in until he starts moving
the bed i am on. i am best friends
with calendula cream. it's part of the
skin care protocol. three times a day
i love up on all of the areas getting
attention. so far, my skin is soft, and
i don't really feel anything different
except when i don't wear the cotton bra
they recommend. lace and this treatment
don't mix. so cotton bras for me for
a bit. i just bought some on amazon.
loving my prime delivery.

my hair is still doing her amazingness.
the standard is that after chemo / and
the cold cap protocol you wait for 3
months, and i'll keep doing the same
care regime as when i was going through
the chemo. that means no color, no cut,
no heat, no brushing except once a day
etc. my hair is like a curly calico cat
right now. so proud of her for staying
on my head—now she is growing and i have
a hair rainbow of brown, gray, caramel,
black, and more! it's spectacular.
culturally it's not on trend, but . . .

she's growing and working hard, and
culturally that is on trend. april 20th
i have a big appointment at germaines
for a cut, color, and love!

i have continued my pilates/gyrotronics,
and i have started to walk for longer
distances (this to me means about 1-2
hours, not the crazy walks i was taking
before) as it keeps everything flowing.
keeping my body happy and connecting to
her needs is new to me. it's part of my
work right now.

i go into dogeared a bit more and have
developed a love for skype on the days
i am not there. i love engaging with
the team and turning my superpowers
into something great for ms. dogeared.

besides that, i am working hard to
keep life simple. (as i write this it
sounds like it's already a problem—ha!)
family, work, and of course me as i re-
engage into the world with balance and
boundaries. last week i gave myself a
"c+" and this week i am on track for
something in the "b" range!

i am still being cared for at an
A++++++ level by my family and friends,

and i am in a good space for more
miracles, growth, and learning.

i love you all . . .

mmc

Subject: me!

hi!

i am through with the main radiation!!!
i have 8 more days of what they call
the booster which is focused on my
tumor site only so it will allow the
rest of the area to heal. my body is
strong and doing her thing. super proud
of all she does to keep me going!!!

love you all.

xxxxmmc

CHAPTER 10

BACK AT THE TABLE

There is a time in the morning that creates the perfect frame for some inner quiet. Cozy in my bed, I gaze at the beautiful trees in my yard, receiving their silent friendship. The sun streams in my window as she's gaining altitude in the sky behind the hill in my backyard. It's soft and safe (no sunscreen required), all while I am cocooned in my blankets, just waking up and checking in on all my parts. Her beams hit my bed and me, and I am transported into this shine for a period of time before she rises too high and has moved from my window onto the rest of the world. It's my own personal sun show, gracing me with the warm optimism of a new day. I am a moon girl, so playing with the sun like this, and being grateful for this time with her, is a growing reverie that wakes up my gratitude gene on most days.

Today I am grateful for my legs that can walk me to this space where I sit to write; my eyes that can see this screen;

my office that is comfortable and pretty; my intention deck (homemade oracle cards that someone gave to me); my water that tastes good and is contained in a glass I love the shape of; my Aquaphor lip balm that is a staple in my life; my Post-it notes that hold many thoughts and ideas; my excellent #2 pencils; the stacks of papers that made up the outlines to this book; the pictures of my kids and husband that make me feel loved; yes, my essential oils and diffuser that work overtime to make my space smell good and support healing; my checkbook that has enough money in it to live a sweet life; my wooden phone holder that Merlin made me with a heart on it; the pretty chair I get to sit in that is covered in a vintage orange kantha fabric; the books surrounding me that have great meaning in my life; an oyster shell that is now an incense holder . . . you get the picture.

* *

PEARLS OF WISDOM

At every ordinary point of contact in our lives,
we can not only feel gratitude,
we can *generate* it.

What does your gratitude look and feel like?
What has the possibility to make
your gratitude list each day?

* *

I always want to spend my time like this.

This, however, is not the feels we got when we came back to Dogeared after healing from breast cancer. They say cancer runs through all parts of your life, so when your life is on fire it's time to take it on—to look at the whole not just the parts, to heal all the way through. That meant Dogeared too.

I was tired after treatment and just wanted to come back to something that felt like I remembered it—stable, purposeful, loving, and strong. Yet things were different as Dogeared had operated autonomously from us for over half a year. Yes, we could have started a gratitude list right then too, and it probably would have served us well, yet our focus was on looking at where we had arrived at with our Dogeared, and to be honest, we didn't use our gratitude practice as much as probably would have benefited us. We had the tool, but just didn't go there.

There had been tremendous growth with seemingly no financial guardrails. Great ideas and talented people without a lot of fiscal responsibility. Many of our core, ride-or-die team members weren't happy. They loved the brand; the challenge had to do with the current energy. We had lost our spirit a bit. The nimbleness that we had always prided ourselves on was not there. We were big and reactive. There was no moderation or balance. Resources felt capped. There was a feeling of contraction even with all the growth.

The question that came again and again to Merlin and me:

How do we take the Dogeared that we love and make it something that feels good again?

I was still healing from all the treatment my body had accepted, and Merlin was very protective of me, wanting to shield me from everything that wasn't about my progress. We had to have some conversations about this, as my learnings along the way made it so I could protect myself, meaning self-care was becoming a top priority for me. This was not what we thought we would be managing, yet it made sense. Cancer had upgraded my relationship with myself, my family, my friends, and so of course Dogeared was due for an upgrade too.

We love our Dogeared. Love what it represents in the world. Love our global community. We love the most that we are a tiny speck in the plus column of someone's life.

Acknowledging those truths for ourselves, we contemplated our next steps. We made some management changes, yet we largely kept doing the same things that had always worked. The difference was the world had changed around us, and we had not joined the party. By this time, there were lots of companies doing what we do. We had created a marketplace and got to be the front-runners with our product line for years. What was our differentiator now? Jewelry placed on cards with messages was everywhere, the competition was big, and we just weren't in a place to keep our win. We were lucky, as we had so much history with our customers that we did keep selling, just not at the rate we had.

Priority one for us was my continued healing. Once you are "done" with treatment there is still lots of follow-up—doctor's appointments, testing, and of course, fine-tuning the support needed to stay in the healing space. This involves the cornerstones of self-care, like proper sleep, exercise, food as medicine, mental well-being, friendship, spiritual connection, and other practices and decisions that work to nourish, not deplete.

We operated like this for a few years. With the focus being mostly on me and my healing, we didn't have the energy to envision and strategize the bold moves needed to compete. We couldn't find our groove.

We had lots of opportunity to sell the company, as potential buyers were inquiring on a regular basis, during our biggest growth periods and even when we were not in growth mode. We would always explore it for a minute and then ultimately decide against it. We just knew that we were going to be the ones to give her the next shot—to figure out how this beautiful energy known as Dogeared would get her reinvention. She was family, and we just weren't ready for our next season of life to not include her.

———◆———

At a certain point, we decided it was time to go back to the basics. Simplify became our mantra. When shedding this kind of history and deciding what stays and what goes—who and what gets a seat at the new table—it is a moment for high-vibration choices. We felt the importance of looking at the whole thing through the lens of a central question: What matters to us now? Interestingly, we liked the money part and not a lot of the rest. The money dance had another new rhythm. One we were ready to explore. We would keep the good and part with the rest in a place of deep appreciation and understanding. Conscious uncoupling, you could say.

We decided to take out everything from the business that did not feel authentic to our next steps. And what were those steps? We were taking the next intended ones and trusting that the path would open. We were in the doing *and* in the being. A little more in the doing at first, while we cleaned and cleared thirty-plus years of whatever needed to move on.

• •

PEARLS OF WISDOM
There's a famous acronym that I like to
keep in view: KISS—formerly known as
"Keep It Simple Stupid." Since I'm not
a fan of the word stupid, how about
forever going forward, it now means:
Keep It Super Simple
Deliver the simplest outcomes that everyone
can understand and use. Less really is more.

• •

The learning, however, was that we weren't broken. We were being called to re-create and rewire, and birth a new vision for what our life could look like with Dogeared leading the way as always. She was our creative playground and bridge-builder—connecting us to people everywhere.

I read an article about a hugely influential urban planner, Jaime Lerner, where he said it best: "You get creative when you take a zero from your budget. But sustainability starts when you take two zeroes from your budget." This became our guiding light. It was the zeroes game for us.

The game got tactical . . . and took time. Divine time. And yet, I wished it would hurry the heck up.

First, we had to face the truth that we did not love the archaic systems we were working in, that the industry works in. We did not like being part of a hamster wheel of logistics going nowhere. And then there were the *processes*. So many processes. Systems that had been customized to the point where they didn't serve us anymore. No one liked them or wanted to use them. Time for a switch. Seems easy. It's not. Sometimes simplicity is not simple at all.

PEARLS OF WISDOM

Technology now has so many offerings.
No need to customize anything too much.
If you must rework or overwork a system,
then it's probably not the one for you.
Out-of-the-box solutions should be just
that. Ready to go and ready to support.

We dumped our big, fancy, expensive, specialized in-house IT system that we had named "Nav." We were nervous about the history Nav held for us, yet spiritually it needed to be gone for us to heal. This broken system had become a giant elephant in the room housed within our own walls. We backed it up and left it to spend time in a storage unit. It was physically and energetically heavy and old, so retirement felt right. We are now using an off-the-shelf system that supports us in a very inexpensive and agile way.

We reviewed our entire product line and took our offerings down from 5,000 styles to about 200. Twenty percent of our styles create 80% of our sales. These are our core best sellers. These styles keep the lights on. Let's allow them to shine, we decided. This was called our "SKU (stock keeping unit) rationalization project" and was like going through old photos from years back. If the "SKU" wasn't bestselling, it did not get to stay. We stopped a lot to discuss the how and why of many jewels. It was a fun project except for the huge spreadsheets involved. Eye fatigue set in, yet hearts were happy as we blessed and moved along thousands of styles.

We chose to do business that could be done with ease. That meant saying so long to almost every major department store that we were in, as well as some big online giants. Making these phone calls, there was sweetness to it as our relationships had grown over the years. And—we were ready to be free from the archaic systems and the constant ask for funding for marketing or store placement—meaning with the bigger multi-store department and chain stores. How many stores could we be in and how much store real estate could our brand get was not where we wanted to be. The striving for "new, new, new" also was a factor, as it went against our core desire and our dedication to the concept of slow fashion. We like to make products that are made to last. We don't want to put things out just for the sake of keeping up with calendars that require more, more, more. Anything that required special packaging or special shipping, we moved away from too. We wanted to do things simply.

We happily kept selling to a handful of local stores and smaller online retailers in the United States and Canada. Long-term relationships that worked. Partners who appreciated our quality, our history, and our business model. Wholesale international business required a lot of hand-holding, so we rarely do it anymore. Instead, we sell directly to customers around the world through our retail dogeared.com site, as the global community is still important to us.

The hardest part of the reboot was saying so long to many team members as we started outsourcing many of our operational needs. Outsourcing meant that we would no longer be running our own warehousing, technology, accounting, and sales, etc., all of which we had been managing in-house, ourselves. This required a lot of management hours, systems, and space—along with the high head count (team members) and expertise to run all of that. All combined, this was not a marker on our compass of simplicity. We chose to work with companies in the United States that were experts in these areas and had turnkey solutions for us.

Happily, outsourcing where it made sense to allowed us to *stop* outsourcing most of our jewelry production. Now we're able to truly monitor our quality and timing. This allows us to ship to our customers everything they order—something we had not been great at for a while. There is no reliance on anyone except us and the small group of artisans we work with to create our jewels. We even rekindled relationships with vendors that we had worked with when the business was beginning. The history we shared with them made this time of transition so powerful.

We sold 20,000 square feet of office/studio space, two buildings right next to each other, as we no longer needed them (a long way from the quirky shire of our earlier days). Big exhale here. It takes a lot of resources to keep two buildings running and maintained. Plus, I think empty buildings take on a heavy energy, even if good vibes have rolled through them for years and years. One of these we sold for a big profit during COVID, which was not the best time for commercial real estate—a time when commercial office space was plentiful and basically being given away, as everyone was working from home. This sale just amplified the fact that when you are on the right path, things will occur that don't make sense, like making a profit on a building when the market was not necessarily handing out big money for commercial space. Divine guidance was in the building!

We donated huge amounts of furniture, office supplies, art supplies, computers, lights, and jewelry, circulating it all back into our community. It turns out that 20,000 square feet of space can hold a lot of stuff! Going through every cabinet, drawer, desk, closet, and attic space was a Marie Kondo super dream. We blessed it all and moved it on. The number of "things" found and blessed was overwhelming at times. How many strands of pearls can one girl have?

Some areas, like the design closets, were a crafters dream. It was cool for us to see what we had created in the design space over the years. So many sketches of designs that never were designed. Beads, gems, fibers, crystals, gold, metal, jewelry tools, notes about what seasons things were for—the unraveling of decades of creativity. Old Dogeared catalogs and marketing pieces. History. Like going through your childhood memories, with stories attached to so many items we encountered.

Money! We restructured some debt, which was hard and not fun. We inherited a lot of it from when we were focused on my healing. Extra not fun. No one likes debt, and for us it's part of the cleanup. I get to practice my money tools and not get caught in the mind chatter or fear conversation. As we know from my previous stories, I have had many a night that included a date with the moon—"Sleepless in Los Angeles" because of the money dance. We were able to get out of some agreements that were not really benefitting our new goals of simplicity. Services that were more for when we had the many facets, the many customers, the many many.

We looked at *everything*. Common sense was our compass. We even scrutinized the cost of doing business in the state of California. We love this place, so this was big. We chose to stay, which is the right decision for right now, as being bi-coastal, which we practiced for a bit and did love, wasn't aligned with other things in our life at play, namely my family. *(California, if you are listening, it's time to make things easier for the businesses that want to be here!)*

We purposefully took our multiple-eight-figure business to a fortieth of the size it was. Yes, we did. From a financial perspective, this is not what most would do. I thought this wouldn't feel as good as it does. This is certainly the kind of situation where the moodiness can pop up, yet the freedom and beauty of where we are headed is where we like to put our attention and time. We are reinvesting in our reinvention.

All in all, this grand cleanup took a few years. We kept finding things that would either make us laugh or cry, which allowed us to practice our "no problem!" approach to work and life.

CHAPTER 11

IT'S A DOGEARED LIFE

Our team now is small and mighty. We all wear a lot of hats. We have our areas of expertise and come together as needed for anything the business requires. The only people with a seat at our table now bring their "A" game. Their talents, their creativity, integrity, and passion give me peace. Some are former Dogeared team members who are excited about what we are doing and have a connection to what was and what will be as we go forward. We sit around the table and design and solve and enjoy all that this Dogeared family is. This "table" is such a symbolic place to launch from—and sometimes it shifts from one location to another. Every now and again, it means we're packaging and shipping from our dining room, which I have a new fondness for. There is a soulful energy there with its well-worn surface and abundant scratches—telltale signs of a life well-lived.

Most of all, I love who is around this table. Oftentimes, I'm designing and strategizing with my daughter from this same space. Recreating with Grace and growing us both. She doesn't know anything but Dogeared, as Dogeared is older than she is. We are present with each other. What's fun is experiencing the Marcia and Grace of the now. We get to draw from the past and its wisdom as a point of reference. Our experiences will be different than before, as we are different than before. It's the now of us!

We have become nimble again. We are in flow again. Foundationally, we are taking on what's next in our evolution. From a place of expansion in our minds and hearts, we found that we needed to restart with contraction. We pulled back, not only to remember the magic of what was sprinkled on our early days of business, but also to see what it feels like now to create from this freshly tended foundation—the timeless ground of awareness, aliveness, and being fully on purpose with thirty-plus years of experience to enjoy.

PEARLS OF WISDOM

For Merlin and me, our deepest feeling
about Dogeared is summarized this way:
We get to do this.
When you approach your life with an
"I get to" instead of an "I have to," the
lens of perception is shifted. It's a gift.
Yes, you "get to" live life like this.

LAKE HOUSE LESSONS (AKA BUSINESS IN THE NOW!)

I can best exemplify where we are hanging out now by sharing a story about our lake house. With Merlin being from the East

Coast, we have always vacationed back there, and when the time was right, we decided to buy a rambling, in-need-of-love-and-care, single-story ranch-style home with the lake as our front yard and sunsets that rocked our world. It was a special place that we came to with family and friends. We thought we would have this treasure in our family forever.

We owned it for years, and once we knew the space and how we liked to live in it, we decided to do a simple remodel (like removing the bathroom that was literally in the middle of the hallway, like a Jack and Jill bathroom in the most insane place) that turned not-so-simple as COVID showed up. Calling it the house that FaceTime built, we smoothed over anything that was not so functional and brought a lot of it up to date. When it was done, it was so easy to be there—true and simple elegance.

During COVID, Merlin and I spent a lot of our time at the house, as no one wanted to see anyone. It was a dream to be there. New England in the fall, and even in the winter. Only the crazy winds might have driven us away. This created some freedom for us to see if being bi-coastal was something we would like to do. We loved it, as it turned out, and enjoyed all that the area and our home had to offer. Being alone with Merlin like this brought us to another level of being us. When we decided to go back to California for reasons of all kinds, we had some intuition that what we had created for ourselves in this time and space would not be something we would enjoy again for a long time. Just a feeling . . . and as we know, we get to trust those inklings.

We decided to rent out our lake house for part of the summer to have it generate income and be used and appreciated when we weren't there. I believe a house likes to be purposeful and in service—just like office buildings, empty houses lose their oomph.

The rental market is incredible on the lake, and the house was rented quickly by many people. One of our renters was a wonderful man and his family. He was athletic, strong, and a lover of the outdoors who also happened to be in a wheelchair. With some added ramping and other accommodations, our house was well-suited for them to enjoy, due to it being on a relatively flat piece of land with an easy ingress into the lake and being single-story with wide rooms. We were thrilled that our house got to serve in this way. They loved it so much that they booked for the next summer too.

Time has a way of revealing what's most relevant, doesn't it? Not too long into this exploration, I discovered that a bi-coastal life wasn't *really* going to work so well. I am lucky enough to have two parents who live a few hours from me in California, and once COVID was a few years in, I realized that me being on the East Coast was not going to be an easy thing after all. I wanted to spend time with them, and I wanted to support their aging process. We could not figure out when we were going to be able to head back east. Life had gotten busy again, and having a house sitting for a year with no energy in it—no life being lived within its walls—was not what we wanted.

Trusting in divine guidance, I woke up one day with a very guided idea, and Merlin and I talked about a "what if" scenario where we would sell the house. The market was hot back there, so we decided to speak to our realtor and see what he thought. The numbers lined up to make us say "yes," so we decided to list it. This wasn't an easy decision, but it aligned with our desire for a simpler life experience, where we could feel freer. We told our real estate agent that we thought our renter might be interested in buying, as we had heard through a few locals that this was the case. We had great interest from lots of people who saw the house, as its lake front is like nothing around. After the first open house, within hours, we got a generous and pristine offer from this man and his family. It came with a letter that spoke of the love they already had for the house and how it just suited them perfectly. We knew it was their house. Merlin and I joked with each other that we felt like we had gotten it ready for them.

It's important to highlight that this real estate deal was one of pure ease and flow, which I had not had in a real estate transaction before. There was so much integrity. We didn't doubt it. Both sides did what was needed to close quickly and make it happen. A few weeks before closing, Merlin went to their house for dinner to meet them in person, and at the end of dinner, he gave them the key to their new home—all this before the papers were signed, as that is how beautiful business can be done. We have since gotten to spend more time with them, and they have even extended us an invite to come stay at the house. This experience has become the litmus test for how we want to move through life *and* business. This is the harmonious arena we want to continue to play in on all fronts, especially with Dogeared.

Talk about Divine Timing doing her thing. The lake house is a shining symbol for us of this ever-present force in our lives. We believe! And we are indeed empowered by trust. Attuning to this concept includes standing back and knowing that when you need it, the characters will appear—and the way forward will be clear to you.

As we keep folding down the pages of our own journeys, Merlin and I feel more vibrant and curious and connected than we have in a long, long time. We recognize the power of believing and dreaming as our own best healers. We're working together to redefine what success feels like and looks like for us.

With that said, our personal narratives can be limiting sometimes, when we find ourselves getting comfortable and complacent seeing ourselves as "this," and not "that." As one thing and not another. To shake things up, I tried option trading recently. Yes, the stock market option trading. Never did I see myself as an option trader. If you were going down a list of things you might check off that I might be, I am sure you would not have picked that. I would not have either. The point is, we are here to try on many versions of ourselves with no limiting beliefs. All you need is the desire to begin. Give your desire a spin and see what comes next . . . *The opportunity to re-invent. Not being attached to outcomes. Taking the next intended steps toward what feels right and good (finding the gold within)—and trusting along the way (forging that unshakable trust!).*

(And in case you are wondering, option trading is so not for me.)

What *unlimiting* narratives are in view for you right now? Mine have a lot to do with coming from behind the scenes to a place that's a little more front-of-house. Here are some things on my next, next list—all requiring me to trust and say so long to any of my limiting narratives.

- This book! (See how powerful trust is?! You're holding this book in your hands!)
- A travel schedule for my book tour, which I believe will be a great way to visit small towns and beautiful bookstores and talk to anyone who has the time to join. (I hope to meet you!).
- More events facilitated by the Healing Bus, with possible new partnerships.
- Maybe some of my book tour will be in conjunction with Healing Bus events and a friend's music tour as that feels aligned.
- Would love some retreat space in New England.

- A meditation practice that is blowing our minds now, which we will continue to explore.
- The documentary that we dream about creating with our friends.
- Learning to play piano and guitar, so I can sing and play along anywhere I am.
- Creating a line of caftans.
- And being open to anything else that may just "appear."

Some of this may land much like I'm envisioning it, and some of it may morph into something completely different. Other ideas may flow in, and some of it may never come to fruition; meanwhile, I'll continue to enjoy leaning into the yin and yang of it all.

OK, my new friend, so what's on your next, next list?

● ● ● ● ● ● ● ● ● ● ● ● ● ● ● ● ● ● ●

The final . . . PEARLS OF WISDOM

This came to me in a recent meditation,
and I believe it was referencing
me finishing this book. ☺
*If you are going to ride the
bike, then RIDE the bike!*

● ● ● ● ● ● ● ● ● ● ● ● ● ● ● ● ● ● ●

With much love, I say so long and thank you for being part of my journey.

Together, let's RIDE!

A FEW THOUGHTS FROM MERLIN

And I get the last word . . .

She bounded out the back door, floating across the driveway to the garage where I was working; the smile across her face and the lightness in her being said it all—*she was flying high!* She had finally summoned the courage to read the first pass of a chapter of this book to her peers, and the positive feedback was everything she needed in that moment. Speaking out loud, hearing her own voice as she read her own work, Marcia had been validated beyond all she could have hoped for. I recognized this glow. It had struck before, some thirty years ago, at the Rose Bowl swap meet in Pasadena, California, where she had created some crafts and pieces of jewelry to sell. She loved selling what she had made. That spark quickly ignited Dogeared and has since taken us on the journey of our life that you have just read about. I suspect this latest spark—*More than Millions*—will not be the last.

I have the best seat in the theater of Marcia's life. Celebrating mostly, sometimes coping, but most importantly just making sure she knows I'm there for her. We both signed up for big lives, and when we met in our twenties, it was a big times two. We weren't on either of each other's vision boards (if that was even a thing in the late eighties), but somehow the moon and stars aligned, and we met at the party Marcia described in Chapter 2. Our versions of our first meeting vary; however, one key element is there in both accounts—handing her a Budweiser. What she didn't say is that I stood in front of the car she was in with no intention of moving until she gave me her phone number, which she scribbled on a piece of paper and threw out the window because she did not want me to be run over.

Just as my Boston accent wasn't the romantic European one she had imagined, she wasn't the short, blonde-haired ballerina in a Jeep from Chicago that I had conjured up. Luckily, she was so much more.

There was a bigger plan in place for us, so when the awkwardness of me having all female roommates and the constraints of Marcia living back at home with her parents mounted, we resolved all of that by moving in together. I knew I could survive on my own. Since high school, I had hitchhiked around the country and landed in Los Angeles with plenty of urban survival skills. So doing this together thing was something new. Another experience.

My family and friends all loved Marcia and would go out of their way to let me know. They saw her beauty. One night, driving to a hockey game with a buddy, the words "You know, I think I'm going to ask Marcia to marry me" came out of my mouth. And there it was: I was thirty years old and had found the woman, the mother of my would-be children, the person I was going to share the rest of my life with. And if you ask her mother, I had found a woman who was way out of my league!

Any concern about living together was quickly muted by the pace of the vibrant, fun, and rich lives we were living—and this was before there were thoughts of little M and M's running around, or even Dogeared.

Continuing to discover who Marcia is, and who we are together as we travel across all kinds of terrain, is the experience I love the most.

———————•———————

Marcia is a smart, strong, powerful woman with equal parts of love and compassion. My wife is a leader among friends, family, and colleagues. She is a rock that is rarely shaken. Since we met, she has used her threads of wisdom and caring to weave a beautiful tapestry that eventually cloaked our family in love and protection. This was our life; this is what we knew.

And then one day, these words, "Yep, there's something there," from the radiologist examining Marcia's breast. We shook, but through her treatments and her inspiring confidence in healing, she *roared*—chasing that tangled, misguided mass of cancer far away from her body. The cancer chapter in our life is now closed, giving all of us a unique perspective and renewed strength.

Having read this far, you know a lot about our love story and a lot more of our lives. Thank you for letting us into your world through these Dogeared pages. Maybe by now, you won't be surprised to know that we're most excited about the pages *ahead* in our story, the chapters not yet written. We know that the wisdom we have accrued and the experiences we've shared have paved the way for what is next.

When Dogeared blew up the inspirational jewelry category, with messages of love and hope, we heard how thousands of people had kept the card their piece was attached to and placed it where they would see it throughout the day—using the message as a touchstone to their jewelry. These conversations continue to this day. Amazing stories of people and their experience with their Dogeared jewelry. It took us a minute to realize what was happening, but we witnessed, learned, and now know it is simply the power of *believing*—believing in goodness, believing in love, believing in yourself . . . the list of how and what to believe in is endless.

With Dogeared as a driving force, the Healing Bus is shifting into gear for people to evidence and explore healing modalities they may have otherwise never experienced. With the power of believing and new paths to wellness, we are embracing the next opportunity to give big. We are entrepreneurs, and we are builders. The last thirty years was just us getting ready for our encore. I'm an alchemist of togetherness—I love making connections, and making good things happen. Together, with Marcia, we will see how far we can go sharing the power of believing, as people discover new paths to their own well-being.

And because I get the last word . . .

A few years out from her cancer experience, Marcia brought fifteen amazing women together, her circle of closest friends and family, to celebrate life. They did a 3-day, 39-mile Avon Breast Cancer Walk. I was in awe of the warmth and connection that they shared—along with the thousands of others who were there, unified in their fight against breast cancer. I wanted

Marcia's band of warriors to know how moved I was by their love and support for my wife, which inspired me to write a poem. Usually, a hike to a waterfall is where I would write a good poem, and this time, although no waterfall was present, the words were just there, needing me to release them . . .

She Roared

I am a strong, powerful man . . .
Cast from the womb of a woman, nourished by the breast of a woman.
This gift, creator of life, I will never know, this human bond, I
will never feel.

I am blessed to know so many women who tap their higher
power, live in strength, join together, lift each other up and with
their collective voice . . . They Roar.

Your message is so strong, your love is so real, the earth shakes,
sending waves of compassion rippling into our needing world.

You walk with purpose and passion. You lead with commitment and
action. And in your wake, you create a world better than you found it.

I am a strong and powerful man . . .
I watch in awe, as the women in my life accomplish the
magnificent every day.

— Merlin

ACKNOWLEDGMENTS

Ms. Dogeared.
Thank you for being the launchpad, the classroom, the playground, and the heart.
You gave me wings and a wild ride, and I've loved (almost) every minute of it.
And now, watching you evolve?
Still surprising me. Still doing your thing. Still so very Dogeared.

Team Dogeared. Past and present—my dream team.
The doers. The believers. The soul-forward humans who poured your hearts into everything.
You created. You cared. And it showed in every detail.
You made magic daily—and you made it matter.

Merlin. My person.
You have walked beside every season—the building, the stretching, the becoming.
We have grown up together, grown wiser together, and learned how to love each other more gently with time.
You hold the history. You hold the future.
Decades in, and I still choose you.
You are the gold at the center of it all.

Mom and Dad.
Thank you for giving us such a strong start, for the love and values that shaped everything.
Now that I'm a parent, I can confirm: You made it look much easier than it actually is.

Grace and Jordan.
Thank you for expanding my heart in ways I never imagined.
You've been my greatest teachers in the school of unconditional love.
Jordan, your courage and independence inspire me in my own choices and life.
Grace, the way you hold Dogeared, and yourself, with such strength and grace makes me proud beyond words.
Watching you both grow into yourselves is pure joy.
I love you to the moon and back.

Stephanie and Mark—my siblings.
What would this season of life be without you?
We've been through it, grown through it, and laughed our way forward.
Life is better (and definitely funnier) with you two.

My golden circles of women. You know who you are.
You have witnessed the pivots, the unraveling, and the rising.
You ask the brave questions. You sit beside me in the hard moments. You celebrate wholeheartedly when one of us shines.
These friendships are treasured.
You hold space. You tell the truth.
You light my way.

You are living proof that the richest parts of who we are are reflected back by the women who walk beside us.

I love us.

The Book Doulas—Kristine Carlson and Debra Evans.

You didn't just help me write a book. You helped me trust that I had one in me.

You midwifed these pages into the world with wisdom, steady hands, and impeccable timing, even when I arrived with more feelings than structure and a desk covered in Post-it Notes.

You believed before I did.

That matters more than you know.

Thank you for helping me find the throughline in the mess and the magic.

Dinner, cocktails, repeats.

The Self Publishing Agency (TSPA)—Megan Williams, Ira Vergani, Danna Mathias Steele, and Kathie Lynas.

Thank you for taking my dream seriously and turning it into something real.

You shepherded this book across the finish line.

And I won.

Mimi Ison.

My Foreword makes me so happy. Thank you for seeing me so powerfully and for reminding me of a time when this journey was just beginning.

You reflected back the magic I sometimes forget is there.

You are a gift—then and now.

And finally—to you, dear reader.
Thank you for saying yes to this book. For holding these pages. For letting my story meet yours.
You showed up. You stayed open.
And maybe—just maybe—you remembered what has been there all along.
The gold's within.
It always was.
Keep going. It's all in there.
And … it's all yours when you're ready.

ABOUT THE AUTHOR

Marcia Maizel-Clarke is an author, speaker, and the founder of Dogeared Jewelry.

After more than three decades leading the company, she was proud to pass leadership to her daughter Grace, who grew up alongside the brand. Marcia now stays connected in an advisory role, sharing perspective, brand storytelling, and lived experience while watching the next chapter unfold through a new lens.

She is in a season of creative exploration—gathering people, mentoring the next wave of makers, and building community in new ways.

Marcia lives in Southern California with her husband, Merlin, where life continues to surprise in unexpected and creative ways.

Here are ways to connect with Marcia:
IG: @marcia_maizelclarke
Newsletter/Blog: dogeared.com/pages/love-mmc-signups
Dogeared IG & TikTok: @dogearedjewelry
Dogeared FB: @dogearedjewelry
Dogeared.com
Dogoodbus.com
Healingbus.org